THE CHURCH AND
THE REALITY
OF CHRIST

THE CHURCH AND
THE REALITY
OF CHRIST

John Knox

HARPER & ROW, PUBLISHERS
New York and Evanston

TO

ABSALOM KNOX

AND

EMMA MANN KNOX

Him whom I see as in a mirror dimly
they see face to face

Contents

Foreword

Christian theology in the present epoch is marked, perhaps most distinctively, by concern for the nature and importance of the Church. There would be no need to indicate all the reasons for this development even if I knew them and were qualified to interpret them; but I do wish to speak briefly of one of them. New Testament scholarship has for a generation been saying in effect: "What we have in the New Testament is a record and reflection of the life and thought of the early Church. This is as true of the Gospels as of the Epistles. What confronts us immediately and directly in the New Testament documents is simply and only the primitive community—what it remembered, what it knew, what it thought, what it felt." We have now become rather familiar with this conception—and at times less sensitive than we should be to its full significance—but it was at first a radically new and a very disturbing idea. We might appreciate the early Church ever so highly, but we were not ready to find the historical foundations of our Christian faith within its life. These foundations, we were sure, were both earlier and deeper. Since, however, there were no other documentary records of them than the New Testament, what knowledge of them could we have if this idea were true?

There are three obvious ways in which we may react to an idea whose truth we cannot reasonably deny, but which seems to threaten some precious security. We can by an act of will reject it (or deceive ourselves into thinking we have rejected it) and thus, with a kind of violence, hold on to our security; or we can grudgingly accept it, yielding up what we are forced to of our security and grasping desperately at whatever vestiges or semblances of it we can salvage; or we may gratefully embrace it, knowing not only that a security depending on the rejection of the truth must be false, but also that a new and disturbing idea, if true, is capable of leading us toward a security more ample and firm than we have known before. The present book is an attempt to set forth one man's experience in seeking to follow, as faithfully and consistently as possible, the leading of the new idea about the New Testament and the Church to which reference has been made.

This book, if I may be allowed to speak very personally, could not have been written earlier in my life—perhaps I should have waited longer still to write it!—but this does not mean that the position it states has been newly, or at any rate suddenly, arrived at. As I look back, it seems to me to have been implicit in all the reflecting I have done on the life and significance of Jesus since my little book *The Man Christ Jesus* was written in 1940. It was more than forty years ago that I first became acutely aware of the problem the present discussion is concerned with—the problem of how faith in Christ can be essentially related to historical fact and yet be as sure as faith must be—and I do not think I have since felt the problem in any greater depth than I felt it then. My first impulse was to say, "If we have only the Church, we have nothing." It took more than twenty years for me to reach the point of seeing that in having the Church we have everything. The present work, then, attempts only to set forth more coherently and, I hope, more intelligibly, a way of conceiving of what God did for us in Christ, which, whether clearly recognized and acknowledged or not, has been expressed in such writing as I have done on the christological theme for many years, if indeed it was not implicit in the particular way I felt the problem itself almost a half-century ago. If my statement of it still lacks clarity, I can only plead the extreme difficulty of putting into words (and thus giving definitive being to) one's most serious thoughts about one's most serious concerns.

The task of the Christian theologian, as I understand it, is primarily a confessional and descriptive one. He is trying to say as accurately and adequately as possible what Christians —that is, sharers in the life of the Church—find true in their common experience. Whether or not this is a fair account of the theologian's task, it indicates what I have undertaken in this book. I have sought to confess and define what the Christian—should I say what one Christian?—knows. What I have written is true or false according as it answers, or does not answer, to the realities of the Church's life as Christians generally, across the world and across the centuries, have known them.

With the permission of the Abingdon Press, I have made some use of materials originally published in an article in *Religion in Life*, XXVII (1958) under the title "The Church *Is* Christ's Body."

I have made no effort to "document" this book with adequate bibliographical references. It ventures to touch on so wide a range of topics that the mentioning of previously published relevant materials (even such of them as I have read), much less any treatment of them, seemed inadvisable. Where I am directly and immediately dependent upon some writer, I hope that I have not failed to indicate that fact in a footnote; and the wider background of reading is indicated somewhat more adequately in a bibliographical note at the end of this volume; but, needless to say, I am greatly indebted to many whose names do not appear anywhere in these pages. The meagerness of bibliographical references generally makes somewhat embarrassing to me the fact that I do allude to several of my own books. In each case I have done so with good reason, that is, in order to avoid repeating explanations

and arguments which I have given with some fullness elsewhere. Still, I wish it were not so.

The first four chapters in this book represent in substance
the Bohlen Lectures delivered in October of 1962. I am deeply
grateful to Bishop Oliver J. Hart of the Diocese of Pennsyl-
vania and to the dean and faculty of the Divinity School of
Philadelphia for my appointment to this distinguished lecture-
ship, as well as for many courtesies.

I am under obligation to a number of friends who have
read parts of my manuscript and given me important sugges-
tions, although the responsibility for the statements of this
book remains entirely my own. These friends are: James M.
Robinson of the Southern California School of Theology;
Evan Williams of Christ Church, Ontario, California; Shunji
Forrest Nishi, Episcopal Chaplain to Faculty and Graduate
Students at the University of California; John M. Krumm,
Chaplain at Columbia University; Daniel D. Williams, Henry
P. Van Dusen, J. Louis Martyn, Robert T. Handy and Cyril C.
Richardson, of Union Theological Seminary, New York City;
David Edman of Christ Church, Bronxville, N. Y.; and W.
Norman Pittenger of General Theological Seminary. To all of
these I am warmly grateful. I want also to thank Marshall D.
Johnson, my research assistant at Union Theological Semi-
nary, for help in checking bibliographical references and in
proofreading.

In all I do I am dependent upon the encouragement and
counsel of my wife. Her help in the preparation of this book
has been particularly important.

JOHN KNOX

I *The Church and the Fact of Jesus*

NO FACT ABOUT THE CHURCH WOULD APPEAR TO BE SO
obvious, and so obviously important, as the relation in which
it stands to the fact of Jesus; and yet few problems are so
baffling as that of defining just what this relation is. By "the
fact of Jesus" I mean the fact that the man to whom the
Church has always referred by that name actually existed and
that he was the particular man he was. Is this fact essential
to the Church's existence, and is the recognition of it an essential ingredient of its devotion and an essential presupposition of its theology? Can we answer this question affirmatively
without surrendering the certainties of faith, putting in their
place what are at best the mere probabilities of historical
fact? But if we answer it otherwise than affirmatively, have
we not cut the objective historical ground out from under
the Church and its message? These three questions both
indicate the essential structure of the problem and suggest
something of its relevance and importance.

The overriding reason for opening our discussion of the
Church with this theme lies, patent enough, in the basic character of the problem. But an added reason for giving first attention to it lies in the central position it has assumed in
current theological discussion. Such conversations as are now
going on in any part of the Church between New Testament
scholars and Christian theologians generally are likely to be

dealing, in one way or another, with this issue. As is so frequently the case, these conversations are proceeding in liveliest fashion in Germany, where Rudolf Bultmann's extreme skepticism as to the possibility of our recovering the content of Jesus' career—and his disparagement of the importance of our doing so even if we could—have provoked the most vigorous controversy. Many distinguished New Testament scholars have declared in various ways their differences from Bultmann, insisting both that we can know more about Jesus than Bultmann has allowed and that this knowledge is indispensable to the existence of the Church. Even more significant perhaps have been the evidences of dissent within Bultmann's own family of scholars. Not a few of these, men who began their careers as his pupils and disciples, are just now expressing, with whatever restraint, their dissatisfaction with views on this particular issue which they had earlier held. They are groping for some way of modifying these views that will not be inconsistent with the general methodological and theological positions of Bultmann, which they see no way of abandoning. Many systematic theologians, recognizing that the controversy is primarily concerned, not with mere facts of history, but with the status and significance of these facts, and that therefore the issue is basically theological in character, have entered the discussion and are taking an increasingly significant part in it.[1]

For all its importance, however, it would be a mistake to suppose that these conversations represent the whole—or anything like the whole—of contemporary theological interest in the general theme or that discussion of it must necessarily have taken its start specifically in reaction to Bultmann's views. The literary and historical criticism of the Gospels, which has been going on for several generations in many parts of the Church, was bound to suggest for any thoughtful Christian not only the question, "How much can we really know about Jesus?" but also the further, more searching

[1] See the bibliographical note on p. 149.

query, "Is this enough? Can we know as much as we need to know?" Moreover, even before Form Criticism established itself, there was widespread recognition of the enormous part which the needs, interests, experiences, and reflections of the primitive Church had in creating the Gospel tradition—the recognition, indeed, that the Gospels, in both intention and fact, are not the product of careful, critical research into the original facts, but are records of the Church's teaching: they bring us Jesus *as the early community thought of him*. The responsible Christian could hardly see and acknowledge this fact without going on to ask, "But what about Jesus as he *really* was? Do I not need to know about *him?*" The problem has been deepened by the recognition, increasingly prevalent among historians generally, of the importance of subjective elements within history itself. Events of the past cannot be seen apart from the response to them—indeed, they cannot be said to exist at all in such isolation. This insight has introduced an element of confusion into the very meaning of the phrase, "Jesus as he really was"—as though there were not already uncertainty and perplexity enough! In a word, skepticism concerning what can be known about the so-called historical Jesus has been widely current in the Church for a generation or more; and although fashions in biblical criticism, like fashions generally, often change, and conservative trends from time to time take over for a while, this skepticism is bound to persist so long as men's minds are free; the grounds for it are too extensive and too real. But the more disturbing doubt is equally unavoidable and has been just as widely felt: "Can our faith, can our whole religious position, be dependent in any vital way upon historical facts so meager and so uncertain?"[2]

[2] This question applies in principle whether we are more "conservative" or more "radical" in our assessment of the historical trustworthiness of the Gospels. I have always felt that I belong at this point among the "conservatives"—that is, I have found myself, as among the Form Critics, nearer in this regard to Dibelius than to Bultmann. I see no reason to doubt that the Gospels bring us a great deal of authentic information

We cannot reflect on this question without realizing almost at once that actually it can and should be asked in a more radical form: Since even the best attested fact of the history of the past can possess no more than a very high degree of probability and since, by definition, Christian and indeed all religious faith must from the believer's point of view be absolutely certain and secure, can faith ever be said to depend upon a historical fact, no matter how well established? Faith must *know* its object in a way we cannot know a historical fact. It is not, it simply cannot be, as tentative, as precariously poised, as our historical knowledge must be. Not all would agree with such a definition of faith. It is often objected that an element of risk belongs ineluctably to religious faith and that therefore the tentativeness necessarily attaching to any historical finding can be acknowledged by the Christian without inner contradiction. I am not prepared to deny that this element of risk exists in faith, although I am myself not nearly so sure as I once was that this is true. I think we may have overworked the idea that faith and doubt belong together as the two sides of a single shield. It may well be that we could not have doubt without faith (since in that case doubt would simply be denial and rejection), but it is not so clear that we could not have faith without doubt, or indeed that faith does not necessarily exclude doubt as light excludes darkness. If this should be true, faith and doubt are associated so closely in our experience, not because faith

---

about Jesus. I have said this in other books; I not only say it again, but also want to insist that the point I am now making in no way gainsays it. I believe that the picture of an actual historical person emerges in the Gospels and that this picture is to a large extent trustworthy. As regards our present problem, however, differences among us in respect to this matter are irrelevant. Once we recognize the character of the Gospels as "Church books," in which such facts about Jesus as they contain can be found only in or under records and reflections of the later Church's interests, needs, and convictions (so that the critical tools of the historian are needed to identify them)—once this happens, we open the door to the indicated question, no matter how comparatively "conservative" our position may be.

involves doubt as a part of itself, but because faith itself is so inconstant and so often feeble and faulty. Looked at in this way, doubt would mean the partial failure of faith, just as shadow means the partial failure of light.

But one does not need to insist on such an understanding of the existential nature of faith in order to meet the objection raised. For even if we recognize an element of risk in faith, it cannot be the kind of risk involved in assuming the accuracy of a historical fact. If there is risk in faith, it must be the absolute, the eschatological risk. We are risking the possibility that the God of heaven and earth will in the ultimate and final reckoning fail to justify our trust in him, not that the chance discovery of an ancient document or a new conclusion of historians could conceivably rob us of it. Are we not forced to recognize that a risk of the latter kind would be intolerable and that in actual fact it does not exist? Whatever risk the believer may be aware of taking—and I am not sure that in the moment of faith he is aware of taking any at all—he certainly knows that he is not venturing anything important on the results of the researches and deliberations of historians.[3] He knows he is not at any vital point dependent upon their findings. How then, he is bound to ask, can he be dependent upon the fact of Jesus?

A related and more general question may now occur to him, namely, the question as to the status, significance, the kind of being which past facts of all kinds can be thought of as possessing. At the beginning of this chapter, in an attempt to suggest the problem we were to consider, I asked,

---

[3] "Faith," as I am using the term, is something more "existential" than Whitehead has in mind when he speaks of "our beliefs" in the following passage, but his words are pertinent at this point, nevertheless: "It is a curious delusion," he writes, "that the rock upon which our beliefs can be founded is an historical investigation. You can only interpret the past in terms of the present. The present is all you have; and unless in this present you can find general principles which interpret the present as including a representation of the whole community of existents, you cannot move a step beyond your little patch of immediacy" *Religion in the Making* (New York: The Macmillan Company, 1926), p. 84.

"Is this fact [that is, the fact of Jesus] essential to the Church's existence, and is the recognition of it an essential ingredient of its devotion and an essential presupposition of its theology?" If we confine our attention strictly to the first part of that question, namely, "Is this fact essential to the Church's existence?" it may be argued that the answer must needs be in the negative. No past fact can be essential to any actual existence. An event or a personality in the past may, as far as we can see, have been an essential factor in bringing the actual existent thing into being; but once it has come into being, the past fact cannot be said to be essential to it. In whatever way essential Christianity is identified, however its essential substance is defined (whether as a Spirit being received, an ethic being followed, a dogma being believed, a cult being practiced, or in any other way), it is an actual present existence, and no past fact can *as such* be said to belong to it, not even the fact of Jesus. To be sure, a particular image of a past fact may belong to the present existence and may be of decisive importance there, but the image is a new, a present, fact, not the past fact as such. A happening of the past, however influential it may have been and however real and important its present consequences, is in itself lifeless and inert. What must be spoken of in the past tense is nonexistent; it was, but it is not. Only in the present tense, or in the present perfect (which may be thought of as the backward extension of the present) can existent things be spoken of. It is in these tenses that we speak of Christ in the totality of his concrete meaning, "the same yesterday and today and forever." But when we refer simply and only to the career of Jesus of Nazareth, we must fall back into the tenses of the past. When we do so, it may be asked, are we not in effect recognizing that however important that career may have been in its own time, our own existence as Christians cannot now be dependent on it?

It is such considerations as these which, as I understand

them, explain the rejection of dependence on "the quest of the historical Jesus," on the part, not only of Bultmann, but also of Paul Tillich. Bultmann finds the historical beginning of Christianity in the "kerygma," the earliest preaching, and in the response of faith to it. "Christian faith did not exist until there was the Christian kerygma; i.e., a kerygma proclaiming Jesus Christ—specifically Jesus Christ the Crucified and Risen One—to be God's eschatological act of salvation."[4] The decisive Event in the past was the original proclamation of this meaning, just as distinctively Christian faith in all the centuries since has been the hearer's positive response to this same proclamation.[5] Tillich speaks of "the picture of Jesus as the Christ," and identifies the emergence of Christianity with the first appearance of this "picture." When a disciple

---

[4] *Theology of the New Testament* (New York: Charles Scribner's Sons, 1951-55), I, p. 8.

[5] The word "Event" is being used here in my sense, not necessarily in Bultmann's. For me the term always designates an actual historical occurrence—a happening in our human space and time and belonging fully and organically to our human history. The Event we are concerned with when we speak of Christ is an "event" in precisely the same sense as the reign of Augustus or the First World War was an "event," however incomparable it may be in actual significance. Bultmann and many other theologians seem often to employ the word to designate a suprahistorical "occurrence"—the "act" of God in Christ, the "entrance" or "inbreaking" of "the Word" into human history. (The term "kerygma" seems sometimes to have this same suprahistorical sense.) To me it seems confusing to use the word "event" to denote this divine "action" as such. I should prefer to say that God's "action" took place in or through the Event—the Event itself being in its totality and in every part a historical occurrence. Because of the intimate relation between this occurrence and the "action"—the *recognition* of the "action" belonging to the actual human substance of the occurrence—it is hard to be absolutely consistent in the use of the word "event," and I do not claim that I have always been so or promise that I shall always be so in this discussion. But what I have said indicates my intention. If ever by the "kerygma" Bultmann means the Eternal Word of God, he is talking about something above history, and no "action" of this Word can *as such* be called a historical event. It seems to me that insofar as he speaks of such an event—that is, of "event" as I am using the term—it was the original proclaiming and hearing (or should we say, hearing and proclaiming?) of the gospel that Jesus was the Christ.

"saw" the saving meaning in Jesus which the term "Christ" designates, the Event occurred.[6] This "picture" obviously does not belong simply to the past. It exists now just as it has been existing; it belongs to the continuing history to which we also belong. The same thing can be said of the "kerygma," or preaching. This is what is proclaimed and believed about Christ and has been proclaimed and believed continuously since the first century. The moment of significant beginning was, according to Tillich, the moment when something which is still being seen was first seen, or, according to Bultmann, the moment when something which is still being heard was first heard. ". . . faith," Tillich writes, "can guarantee only its own foundation, namely, the appearance of that reality which has created [and still creates] the faith."[7] In the immediate neighborhood of this "appearance" in history undoubtedly lie certain incidents and circumstances which can be spoken of only in the past tense. Historians as such will be interested in recovering these surrounding and more or less closely related happenings and circumstances; but so far as Christian theology and devotion are concerned, such researches, while not without a certain importance, will seem, to those whose general position I am describing, at every vital point irrelevant.

Those who share this position—and I am speaking here, not of Bultmann and Tillich only or even of their disciples, but of a wider company, who may differ from one another at many points just as Bultmann and Tillich differ from each other —these will see that whatever importance for history Jesus' life and words have lies, not in what he did and said simply as such, but in what he was seen and heard to do and say; not even in what he was simply as such, but in what he was known to be; and if this is true, we are no longer able to locate the Event in the deeds and words in their simple objective factual-

---

[6] *Systematic Theology* (Chicago: University of Chicago Press, 1957), II, esp. pp. 97-180.
 [7] *Ibid.,* p. 114.

ness. This factualness is not to be denied. One may argue that however uncertain we may be as to what Jesus said and did, he certainly said and did *something*, and that it is this "something" which is decisively important, even though it may not have been witnessed or any significance found in it, and inaccessible though it may be to us. But one may argue so only if one is thinking of an "importance" outside history. If the Event we are discussing is a historical event, if the revealing action of God we are concerned with took place in history, it would be more precisely accurate to say that its importance lies in its having been seen than in its having been done, in something heard than in something said—that is, if one has to say the one thing or the other. Hence the emphasis implied in Tillich's "picture" and Bultmann's "kerygma."

Actually, however, we do not want to say "the one thing or the other." Indeed, those by whom the historical revelation has been received are bound to say both things: that what they have seen they saw *done* and that what they have heard they heard *said*. Acknowledging as they may do the importance of meaning in history, they still cannot forget that the "meaning" is the meaning of *fact*. It is for this reason that those who share, or are sympathetic with, the general position which I have been trying to describe, nevertheless find it impossible to rest in the conclusion as to the status of the fact of Jesus which that position seems logically to involve. This, I should say, is quite as true for Bultmann and Tillich as for the rest of us, although one might wish sometimes for a clearer acknowledgment of it. We cannot relegate Jesus to the background of the Christ Event. It belongs to our existence as Christians to affirm the actuality of Jesus' existence—and not merely the bare fact of it, but something of the full, distinctive quality of it. How can this be true in view of the existential certainty of faith, on the one hand, and the tentativeness of all historical findings, on the other? This is the dilemma into which we appear inexorably to be driven.

The solution of this problem—or, at any rate, an approach to a solution—lies, it seems to me, in our recognizing, and accepting fully and without reservations of any kind, the radical significance of the early Church. For many of us the problem first came to exist when we saw for the first time that it is this Church, rather than events lying back of it, with which the New Testament puts us directly in touch. We need now to see that the Church's priority is not only epistemological, but actual; that the basic, objective, historical reality underneath, and presupposed in, all primitive confession—picture, kerygma, or whatever else—and the actual carrier of all the meanings being confessed was the early Church; and that, in consequence, the only adequate way to define the Event is to identify it with the Church's beginning. We need to see this meaning of the Church with our minds and to embrace it in our hearts. If God acted in history, as we affirm he did, he acted to bring this social community into being. The historical Event to which all distinctively Christian faith returns is not an event antedating the Church, or in any sense or degree prior to it, but is the coming into existence of the Church itself.[8] To be sure, this "coming into existence" must not be thought of as a momentary or "simple" happening. It involved a complex interaction of persons, incidents, and circumstances over a period of time. But if we are asking what gives their characteristic significance to all of these factors, binds them together, provides the "form" in which they have

---

[8] What I mean by "the Church" will emerge clearly enough in the course of this discussion, and some effort at more precise definition will be made toward the end of the book. The reader will see even now that I am referring to an actual historical community—not a merely ideal or eschatological reality—but he will soon gather also that I am not identifying it with any single organization of Christians or with any particular institutional arrangement. In the immediate context, I am speaking of the primitive Church, the community of response to Jesus and to all that happened in connection with him, the community which produced the New Testament. "The Church" is *this* Church and its authentic succession in history. This theme will again be touched on later in this chapter, but anything like adequate discussion must wait till Chapter VI.

their being as historical event, then, I am suggesting, we can be content with no answer less inclusive than the coming into being of the Church.

I have just said that the Event was not a momentary or simple happening. And perhaps, before going further, we should pause to consider this character of it. It is obvious that exactness is not possible in the definition of the content of any historical event. One may define it more or less narrowly. Elsewhere I have described the Event of Christ as including the personality, life and teaching of Jesus, the response of loyalty he awakened, his death, his Resurrection, the receiving of the Spirit, the faith with which the Spirit was received, the coming into being of the Church.[9] These are not items in a chronological series. It is clear, for example, that the personal character of Jesus, as well as his disciples' response to him, must be thought of as a constant, pervasive feature, and I am now pointing out that the "coming into being of the Church" is a way of referring to the essential character of the whole Event. Still, these items do imply a certain temporal duration in the Event. This "duration" might be indefinitely extended. One might think of the Event in such a way as that the Old Testament history would belong to it as well as the entire later history of the Church. It is not only plausible to argue, but it is also both important and true to say, that when Israel first became conscious of itself as the people of Yahweh (not to mention some possible earlier time) the Church had begun to come into existence and that it will not be fully itself until the final fulfillment of all things, to which the Christian looks forward in hope. Although the eschatological dimension may not be present and certainly will not be present in the same way, a similar indeterminateness belongs to any historical event. Who will say exactly when the French Revolution had its earliest beginning or when Rome began to "fall"? And can either of these events be said to

[9] *Jesus: Lord and Christ* (New York: Harper & Brothers, 1958), p. 217.

have "ended" at any particular time, if indeed at all? Does any event in the strict sense ever begin or ever end except with the beginning and end of history itself? Probably not. Events are the stuff of history; and history is a living, organic process, in which every part participates in the whole and the whole is present in every part.

And yet the meaning of history is not merely diffused; it is focused with varying degrees of intensity and with various degrees and kinds of relevance in particular moments. For this reason we are not mistaken in feeling that events can be located and dated, however accurate or inaccurate any given dating may be. To say that the French Revolution occurred between 1789 and 1799 does not mean ignoring its participation in much (perhaps all) that went before it and that came, or will come, after it. So to affirm that the "Christ Event" occurred in the middle years of the first century in close connection with the public career of Jesus does not mean denying that all the experience of ancient Israel and all the experience of the later Church in a real sense belong to it, and it to them. But, on the other hand, to affirm the latter does not mean denying that all this experience had a center or focus, which can be more specifically located or defined.

The point I am concerned to make just now, however, is that this center or focus itself has some temporal extension. The Event, even in the narrowest possible sense, was a process moving toward and reaching a denouement, and must not be limited to the denouement itself. The Church did not come into existence overnight, as it were, or on the day of Pentecost —the career of Jesus being then completed and in the past. It was coming into existence during the whole progress of that career; the process of the Church's "becoming" included the career and much besides. Indeed, for all its integrity and intrinsic greatness, the career has historical significance, even historical being, only because it belonged to the larger whole. The "becoming" of the Church alone gives a unified meaning to the career together with all that happened in connection

with it. In a word, it was the fact that the Church was being
born which made the Event in its totality and in its every part
the particular event it was.

Perhaps an analogy will be useful. If one were asked to
define the phrase "the American Revolution," I believe one
would naturally reply in some such way as this: "The American Revolution was the event which issued in the emergence
of the American nation as an independent state." Now this
means more than that the independent state was the consequence of the Revolution; rather, the realizing of the independent state *was* the Revolution. At any time during the six
or seven years in which it was in progress, no matter what
might have been occurring at the moment, if the question
had been asked, "What is happening?" the true answer (however hidden then or uncertain) would have been: "The United
States of America is being born." If the new state had not
emerged, the situation would not be that the event had not
had its expected or hoped for *result,* but rather that the event
had not occurred at all. Something would have happened, to
be sure; we might still have had Thomas Paine and Patrick
Henry, Washington and Jefferson, Gates and Cornwallis, the
Boston Tea Party, Bunker Hill, Saratoga, and even Yorktown,
but whatever name might have been given to the historical
happening or development to which these items would have
belonged, it would not have been the American Revolution.
Without the achievement of the independent state—the particular independent state which was in fact achieved—that
event would not have occurred. But it is equally true that
granted this achievement, however different may have been
the actual incidents of the struggle, the event *would* have
occurred. Under these conditions, we are not only justified in
saying, but we are logically required to say, that the event in
its formal character *was* the achievement. The American Revolution *was* the coming into being of the independent American state.

Analogies are dangerous because there is always the likelihood of their being pressed farther than is proper or has been intended. In the present case I have in mind only the clarification of the definition of the Event of Christ. The Church, like the nation, traces its origin to an event which only its own existence has made historically significant. Disregarding the remoter beginnings, we may say that this Event began when Jesus first drew disciples around him, that it was in progress during the months or years of his life with them, and that with his death and Resurrection it reached its culmination—the Church, which had been in process of becoming all along, now clearly emerging as the distinctive, self-conscious community it was and is. Moreover, just as one who speaks of the American Revolution will attribute to it just that significance or importance which he finds in the American nation, so we attribute precisely that meaning to the Event which we find, either as reality or as promise, within the Church—no more, no less, and no other. This being true, must we not say that the Event we are concerned with, the only Event we can be crucially concerned with, is simply the historical beginning of the Church itself?

Such a conclusion is bound to encounter at least three objections. First, we are likely to shrink from it because it seems to involve a devaluation of the Event—the Church is so human an affair. But such, we must remember, every historical thing must be! What the Christian affirms is not that a divinely perfect historical event occurred—such a statement would involve a contradiction in terms—but that in and through a historical event in its full, concrete human character, God acted for us men and for our salvation. It is not something in the factual content of the historical occurrence which constitutes its uniqueness, its supreme eschatological importance, but rather this divine action. Just as any "common bush" may be "afire with God," and is not less a common bush for being so, and just as God sometimes makes of some quite natural, even ordinary, happening in our personal lives a moment of decisive, creative significance for us, and yet without denying or modifying a single natural, ordinary fact in it, so we must think of him as acting in history.

As Christians we affirm an Event in our human history in which God supremely revealed himself. We cannot expect to find the evidences of this extraordinary meaning in the factual content of the Event, the circumstances or incidents which comprise it, in any one of them, or in all of them together. To be sure, this has not always been recognized. The Church, finding itself in being and realizing the values belonging to its existence—what it remembered, what it knew, what it hoped for—instead of being content to say what alone it really knew, namely, "God has done this!" sought to locate God's decisive action earlier and more specifically, as, for example, in the supernatural birth of Jesus or in some other miraculous incident or circumstance of his career. But in doing this kind of thing we of the Church are seeking what by definition cannot be found: a source of meaning within history which can exist only beyond it. We are seeking in the form of extraordinary historical occurrences the explanation of what can only be referred to God himself, whose revealing and redeeming action might conceivably take place in or under or through any historical event. Since we actually know this action of God only in the Church, is it not simplest to identify the Event with the birth of the Church? Indeed, what ground do we have for identifying it in any other way, and why, after all, should we seek to do so?

In the second place, it may be objected that the proposed definition of the Event subordinates Jesus to the Church in an intolerable way. "Surely," someone says," the Event was in actual fact dominated by the person and career of Jesus. It happened around him and, so far as any human explanation can go, *because* of him. He was the central, the decisive fact in its occurrence. In identifying the Event with the beginning of the Church rather than with the career of Jesus, you succeed, to be sure, in placing beyond even theoretical doubt the fact of its occurrence; but you purchase this assurance too dearly: you have emptied the Event of its significant content." I shall not now attempt an adequate answer to this objection. This whole book is, in a way, my answer to it. But let me deny at once that to define the Event as I have done means "emptying" it of any of its "content." A definition of essential character and a description of content are two quite different things. When we define the American Revolution as the coming into existence of the American nation as an independent state, we are not denying or overlooking the actual personalities, incidents and circumstances, important and less important, which together comprised it; rather, we are seeking to specify what gives unity, coherence and historical meaning to all of these component elements, what makes them in their totality and interrelatedness a historical event and, moreover, the particular historical event they were.

In the case of the "Christ Event," as the next chapter emphasizes, the content of it is dominated by Jesus—dominated in a way and to an extent which cannot be asserted of any other event in human history. But what *was* the event which he thus dominated? In what did it essentially consist? One cannot answer that it consisted simply in his own person, in his being the unique individual he was. A person simply as an individual is not a historical event. No person, however extraordinary he may be, has historical existence, much less historical importance, except as an element in a more inclusive whole—a cluster of concrete and ideal factors belonging organically to the process of human history—what we are calling an event. It may be argued that, in virtue of who and what he was, Jesus would have been important even if the Church had not come to be; but this means only that he would have been an element in some other event, involving a quite different constellation of forces and factors—that is, if by "important" one means *historically* important. But is it not clear that the Event to which he and his career *actually* belonged was the emergence of the Church? Can anything else in history be pointed to instead?

The third objection to this identification lies in the ambiguity of the word "church." Robert E. Cushman concludes a critical article on the general idea of defining the Event as the coming into being of the Church with the simple question, "Which Church?"[10] He is asking whether we can identify the Event with the emergence of the Church if the Church itself cannot be identified. There is no denying the seriousness of the challenge with which this question confronts us.

At first thought, perhaps, it might appear possible to meet it by saying: "When we speak of 'the Church,' we mean the primitive Church, the Church whose existence is directly reflected in the New Testament writings. It is *this* Church whose birth constitutes the 'Christ Event.' " But tempting as such an answer might be in providing an easy escape from the challenge of Dr. Cushman's question, we cannot avail ourselves of it. To be sure, the Church which came into being was the *primitive* Church. As we shall have frequent occasion to see, this fact means that the experience and thought of the primitive Church have a normative significance which the experience and thought of the Church in no later period can have. The recognition that this is true accounts for the formation of the New Testament Canon and for its continuing authority. It explains our being able to assert that nothing can belong essentially to the Church which was not present in the early Church and is not therefore to be found in the Canon. All of this is true and it is important, but even so, we cannot define "the Church" as being simply and only "the primitive Church" or "the New Testament Church" without relegating it as definitely to the past and thus putting it as certainly beyond the reach of our knowledge as the so-called historical Jesus may be judged to be. The life of "the Church" would then become itself only an object of research, to be recovered, through the use of historical science and imagina-

[10] "Christology or Ecclesiology?" *Religion in Life,* XXVII (1958), p. 526.

tion, only as surely and fully as it is ever possible to recover such past facts. But actually this is not the case. The Church reflected in the New Testament documents is not the *primitive* Church only, but is the Church I know. As I read the passages in which its distinctive life is most clearly expressed, my primary experience is not that of *learning* something about the past, but of *recognizing* something in the present. In a word, the Church is one, not only in space, but in time—the one because the other. If this were not true, it could not be "the Church" at all or have anything like the significance we are ascribing to it.

This acknowledgment leaves us entirely open to the challenge, "Which Church?" It is nothing less than the issue whether what can be called "the Church" exists or has ever existed, for the Church's unity and its existence are bound inseparably together. This is what makes "our unhappy divisions" so intolerable—the threat they pose to the very being of the Church. And yet it is just as certainly true that we can know this threat only because we sense the reality of the Church as an existing fact. The divisions are felt as a peril to the security of what we know, not as a barrier to our achieving or obtaining what we merely wish for. The reality of the Church is always presupposed. I hope that this book will have the effect of clarifying and reinforcing this presupposition, and the final chapter will be largely devoted to an examination of it. Meanwhile, may I say only that I cannot conceive of any form of Christian faith which could exist in the absence of it. Whether we think of the Church as identical with some denomination or group of denominations or as a more inclusive community hidden under our divisions and to some extent denied by them, I should say that to lose the sense of the reality—that is, of the actual existence—of the Church would be to lose the only conceivable ground for any distinctively Christian affirmation about anything. We may have some knowledge of God in our solitariness or through some other social or cultural medium, but our knowledge of God in Christ—of God as acting in and through the particular historical Event—can reach us only through the historical community. If we decide that we cannot affirm the integrity, and therefore the existence, of this community, we destroy our only ground for affirming the Event. This is true, not only because of the way our *knowledge* of the Event must reach us, but also because the Event itself was nothing other than the coming into existence of this same community.

To the consideration of some of the implications of this identification, the succeeding chapters in this book will be given. But before this chapter ends, something must be said about the bearing of this identification on the problem of the status and significance of the fact of Jesus, although this too must wait for anything like adequate discussion. What can be said now is that the proposed identification sets the problem in a different perspective from that in which it stands when the Event is identified simply and only with Jesus and his career or with the beginning of the "kerygma" or the "picture," and that it opens the way to a more viable solution.

This is true, first of all, because the Church is a solid historical reality, and its beginning, an indisputable historical fact. Although belonging to the past, it does not belong to the past only; it is also a present, an existent, fact, and therefore is not subject to the fortunes of historical discovery and the findings of historical research in the way events must needs be when our knowledge of them can be derived only from documents or other "objective" evidence. As we have seen, the same thing can be asserted of the "picture" and the "kerygma," but it is sounder to affirm it of the Church, not only because both picture and kerygma presuppose the Church's existence, but also because both would be mere verbalizations or abstractions apart from it. The "picture" is the Church's picture, and the "kerygma" is the Church's kerygma. This does not mean merely that the picture exists only for the eye of the Church and that the kerygma has historical being only on its lips or in its ears—although these statements are true—but also that the content of both picture and kerygma is provided only by the content of the existence of the Church itself. If the Church had not come into being, there would have been, so far as we can know, nothing of significance to see or to hear or to proclaim. The Church did not come into existence as a response to the kerygma (assuming the kerygma to mean an actual historical proclamation); rather, the proclamation came about because of the Church's new existence and the values realized there.[11] The Church did not come to be because men saw the picture; rather, the picture was what men saw when they became involved in the existence of the Church. Those who emphasize the historical rootlessness of the kerygma in and of itself are mistaken, I should say, in seeking for the roots in the so-called historical Jesus.[12] The historical roots lie closer at hand in the solid historical existence of the early Church.

[11] It is worth noting that in the first two chapters of Acts we hear of the Church's commissioning, of its earliest constituency, of where it met, of its worship, of its receiving of the Spirit, even of its selection of a successor to Judas as one of its leaders—we hear of all of this before we are told of any preaching. The preaching, when it does occur, has the form of an "explanation" of the observed realities of the Church's life. "Devout men from every nation," confronted by what was happening in the Church, "were amazed and perplexed, saying to one another, 'What does this mean?'" It was to answer this question that "Peter, *standing with the eleven,* lifted up his voice and addressesd them." Without the prior existence of the community, Peter would have had neither occasion to preach nor "text" to preach on.

[12] W. D. Davies, for example, speaks of the "kerygma" of Bultmann as "an event hanging in mid-air, as it were, a phenomenon in a vacuum" ("A Quest to be Resumed in New Testament Studies," *Union Seminary Quarterly Review,* 1960, p. 91). But I should say that a not dissimilar judgment can with greater justice be pronounced on the quite different "kerygma" of which C. H. Dodd speaks in *The Apostolic Preaching and Its Developments* (London: Hodder & Stoughton, 1936)—a "kerygma" consisting largely in a series of historical statements about Jesus' career, namely, his Davidic descent, his birth, his preaching and miracles, his death and Resurrection. These historical items, rather definitely fixed and even neatly arranged within an eschatological frame, are held to have comprised the substance and pattern of the apostolic "preaching." The unity

Perhaps the point will be clearer if we take an example from one of Bultmann's most able critics. Joachim Jeremias writes:

> The very heart of the kerygma lies in the words "died for our sins according to the Scriptures." An historical event is implied here: this death happened for us. But this raises the question whether this meaning of the crucifixion of Jesus has been arbitrarily impressed upon the event, or whether there was some circumstance in the event which caused this meaning to be attached to it. In other words, we must ask: did Jesus himself speak about his impending death, and what significance did he attach to it? This question takes precedence of all others; it is vital for faith.[13]

We can agree that the statement "He died for our sins according to the Scriptures" belonged to the primitive preaching. We can also agree that this statement implies a historical event. But from this point on, Jeremias' words seem far less relevant and true. When we say, "He died for us," we are not making a statement about the so-called "Jesus of history," thought of as antedating the Church. We can say "He died" about *that* Jesus, but not "He died for us." The latter fact, if we have any ground for regarding it as a fact at all, is a fact, not merely about Jesus' existence, but about the Church's. To say that its truth depends upon something Jesus said or thought and that therefore a question of past fact, to be answered only through historical research, "takes precedence of all others"

of the New Testament is found in the prevalence throughout it of at least traces of this formal recital, and the truth of the New Testament is found in the truth of the facts which the recital contained. But insofar as this "kerygma" is making factual statements about the past which have no being or ground or validation in the actual present existence of the Church, I should say that it is much more obviously detached from reality than is the "kerygma" in the other sense. It may not be "hanging in the air" above us, but it is encased in the history behind us (what I understand some German writers to mean by *Historie* as distinguished from *Geschichte*), and is therefore separated from us and from our history in a way that the "picture" of Tillich and the "kerygma" of Bultmann are not.

[13] *Expository Times*, (LXIX) (1958), p. 336.

and is "vital for faith" is to misunderstand the nature of both
history and faith. To recognize that the ascription of atoning
significance to the Event has its ground in the actual existence
of the atoning community is not "arbitrarily" to "impress" a
meaning "upon the event," as though an event could happen
in a social vacuum. The community and the Event belong
inseparably together. The Event *was* the community becoming
its characteristic self. And the historical ground of the
kerygma under all its aspects was the community's existence.
My point here is that this ground is solid and indisputable.

As the kerygma and the "picture" have their reality, their
locus, and their validation in the being of the early Church,
so what we have been calling the fact of Jesus has there, and
only there, not only religious and theological significance, but
also existential truth. We have seen that Jesus cannot be
thought of as simply antedating the Church, as being in the
past when the Church began. The Church did not spring *de
novo* into existence after Jesus' career had ended. This does
not need to mean that he "founded" the Church or even fore-
saw it. Arguments about Jesus' conscious relation to the
Church can never be conclusive because of the ambiguity of
the Gospel evidence. But that whole issue is largely irrelevant.
The important thing is not what Jesus intended or expected,
but what God did. And it is clear that God actually created the
Church around and through the career of Jesus. The fact of
Jesus belongs to the process of the Church's "becoming," not
to some prior event or development.

Moreover—and this is the immediately relevant point—
this fact continues to belong there as something, or better as
someone, remembered. I have said that a past fact is as such
dead and inert; but one's past can be remembered, and an
event or a person thus remembered has a kind of being,
whether the memory be an individual's or a group's. I am
not referring, strictly speaking, to a *fact* (which may be
regarded as a mere abstraction), but to the *substance,* the
felt quality, of the past, held in memory in all its concreteness.

Such remembrance belongs essentially to the character of history. Just as it is in the nature of individuals to remember, and their distinctive individuality and integrity are constituted in no small part by their memories, so historical communities carry in their bodies living memories of the past and would cease to be themselves if these memories should in some way be destroyed. This kind of corporate memory—its reality and its importance—receives in the next chapter the fuller consideration it deserves. Meantime, however, I suggest that it provides the clue to the solution of our problem of how a past fact can in any true sense be essential to a present existence. Jesus is *remembered* in the Church, and has been from the beginning; and this memory is deeply constitutive of its being. Tillich and Bultmann are right in recognizing that the actual human Jesus of Galilee and the first century can exist now only as an image in men's minds and hearts. But they fail to recognize—or, at any rate, to attribute sufficient importance to the fact—that the image is of the characteristic kind that belongs to memory and therefore carries in itself, for those who hold it, the assurance of its own authenticity.

I am not sure I can see how historical research could conceivably destroy this memory; but I *am* sure that if it, or anything else, should do so, it would also destroy, or would have destroyed, the Church itself—and therefore, it should be noted, the picture and the kerygma as well. On the other hand, historical research could not conceivably create the memory or anything to take its place. The remembered Jesus, whom the Church has and must have, is not the historical Jesus for whom we make our "quests," whether "new" or "old." Nor is the Church dependent at any vital point upon such researches for the verification of its memory. Whatever may be said about our knowledge of the circumstances of Jesus' life, the Church's intimate remembrance of the man himself is inalienable, and for the Church itself indubitably secure. We have referred to the early community's confession of Jesus as the Christ; but this was not its whole confession, or even, possibly, the more important part of it: Jesus was *Lord* and Christ. The term "Christ" designates principally an understanding or a judgment; the term "Lord" expresses something more concrete: the community's remembrance of Jesus and the continuing, though transformed, personal relationship with him after his death. We touch here on the meaning of the Resurrection, which falls outside the strict limits of this chapter; but even now it is pertinent to observe that the experience of the risen Christ implies necessarily the continuing remembrance of the human person. The significant thing was not that *someone* had risen from the dead, but that *Jesus* had—and the only meaning the word "Jesus" could have had was the remembered person. This memory of Jesus lay deeper in the Church's existence than any conception or belief. It belonged indeed to the existential substance which all distinctively Christian conceptions and beliefs were attempts to rationalize or explicate. It was, and is, an essential element in the very being of the Church.

In such a view, the man Jesus is not relegated to a position of unimportance or irrelevance; but, on the other hand, we are not forced into the position of depending upon pre-Church or preconfessional data, which have to be established by documentary or other evidence. The Church *remembers* Jesus; and, without ceasing, or having ceased, to be itself, it cannot be convinced, either by theologians that this memory is not important or by historians that it is not in all essential respects secure. The "picture," the "kerygma," and the "fact of Jesus" are all empty, abstract and rootless apart from the substance, the concrete fullness, the firm reality of the Church, to which all three belong. Only when we define the Event as the emergence in history of this new community, with all that belonged to it (including its memory of Jesus himself), can we ascribe to the Event all the rich meaning we have actually found in Christ.

II *The Church and Its Memory*

I HAVE VENTURED THE ASSERTION THAT IT IS IN THE CHURCH'S memory that the earthly human Jesus has present reality and that this reality is as important, as surely indispensable, for the Christian as the memory of him is essential to the being of the Church itself. This assertion, I recognize, raises a number of serious questions and calls for both explication and defense. Can we speak truly of the Church's "memory"? Is there such a thing as corporate remembrance? Is not any picture of Jesus we may have either derived entire from the Gospels (in which case it contains nothing new) or else constructed in whole or in part out of the imagination (in which case it contains nothing new that is also known to be true)? If this question should be answered satisfactorily and the possibility and the actual existence of the Church's memory should be allowed, we should still need to ask: What does this memory contain? In what relation does it stand to the Gospels and what bearing does historical research have on it? And, in view of the fact that we have the Gospels in any case, can this memory be said to have the essential, constitutive character in the nature of the Church with which my assertion invests it? These are some of the questions we must now consider.

Of these, certainly the most challenging is the question whether we can properly speak of the Church's "memory."

37

Memory, it may be held, cannot in any literal or realistic sense be attributed to a group. It is essentially an individual faculty. One can remember what one has done or said or has seen or heard; one cannot "remember" what has happened to another. It is obvious, the objector will concede, that an individual's memories of his own past are an essential element in his integrity, even his identity. It is clear, too, that a certain image of Jesus is essentially a part of the Church's existence. But we cannot, except in a poetic if not rather sentimental sense, refer to this image as a "memory" of the Church. There is, and there can be, no such thing.

How can this challenge be answered? In the present discussion we are concerned only with the Church's memory (not with group memory in general), and I shall be seeking to establish its existence and importance by appealing chiefly to the Church's own nature and experience; but a few words at least may appropriately be said in comment upon the broader question.

This is really the question whether it is possible for one individual to share in another's memories. Let it be acknowledged at once that if such a sharing means that one remembers what has happened to another *in the same way* one remembers what has happened to oneself, then the answer to the question is obviously No—and, to anticipate a little, I hope no one will suppose that I am arguing that I can remember Jesus in the way Peter or John or Mary did. At the same time, it seems to me unrealistic to deny that intimate human association involves what can only be described as a sharing in one another's memories. I should say, for example, that my wife shares, to a degree and in a certain sense, in my memory of my father, whom she never saw and who died before our life together began. This does not mean that she could be said to "remember" any of the facts about him—his appearance, his words, or his actions—much of this I too have forgotten. But his reality as a person is present to her in something like the same sense in which it is present to me.

It would be inadequate to say that she is aware of my father's existence only by hearsay. A denial of his existence would seem to her to be a denial of something intimately and surely known, very much as it would seem also to me. And this is true because she knows more than the few facts I may happen to have told her about him; she has an immediate contact with, an intimate knowledge of, my own vivid remembrance of him. In knowing me she knows this remembrance in the same concrete, existential way she knows me. May it not be said, then, that she shares this remembrance with me?

If I may take another example from my own experience, I believe it would be true to say that I share in memories of the American Civil War as its impact was felt in the southern states. I am not referring to such knowledge as I may have of dates and generals and battles—this was derived from textbooks or from some other form of hearsay. But I have knowledge of another, more concrete, kind. My father, although he did not speak of it often, carried in his memory the grim, dark days of the South's defeat and prostration. And *I remember his memory.* I say it in this way because thus it was and is. I remember more than the facts he may have imparted or the illustrative anecdotes he may have told —indeed, these I have almost entirely forgotten. What I really remember is his memory. The original, concrete meaning of the experience of defeat became present to me through what can only be called my father's sharing his remembrance of it with me. And in this case it may be significantly added that, inasmuch as he himself had been born only after the war had ended, his own remembrance was in large part the result of his sharing in turn in the memory of his father and indeed of the whole generation which had actually suffered the war's agony and the final desolation.

This participating in the memory of another, it is important to note, is more than having a lively impression of the character or quality of an event in another's past; one also has a lively impression of its truth, of its having actually occurred.

Works of art may bring us vivid images; and an image embodied, say, in a painting or sculpture may sometimes have its source in the memory of the artist. But in such a case there is nothing in the work itself to tell us so. If we are aware of the origin in memory, we have learned of it in some extraneous way. So far as we can know from the painting or sculpture itself, it may just as well represent the artist's impression of a present model or scene, or record or express a purely imaginary vision. But in such cases the question of factual truth is irrelevant; without regard to it we may enter fully into the artist's experience and share truly in what he sees. But when I say that my wife shares in my memory of my father, I mean not only (or even chiefly) that she has in some measure the same concrete impression of him that I have, but that she has this impression as belonging authentically to memory. She intimately and surely knows that I not only think of him or visualize him in such and such a way, but that I *remember* him so. In the same way, as I reflect on my impression of the southern tragedy of a century ago, I realize that the essential character of the image I have of it consists not simply (or even primarily) in its being a vivid, lively image, but in its being an image of something *remembered* and therefore of something which was indubitably known to have occurred.

Such memories constitute much of the conscious, and even more of the unconscious, integrity of organic groups of men, from families to nations. A "community" is by definition a "sharing," and such memories form an important part of the substance in which the sharing takes place. And, so far as inner existence is concerned, it is the uniqueness of its memories which more than any other factor distinguishes one community from another. Common memories are perhaps the principal element in human cohesiveness—more important than common thoughts, common desires or common hopes. It is often pointed out that in Soviet Russia the effort to build community on ideology has been only partly successful; the people have proved to be more deeply Russian than Soviet.

They may *think* as Soviets, but they *remember* as Russians. Sometimes, as I reflect on the contemporary struggle of the Negro and white peoples of the American South toward a more ample community, I think of how important the memory of slavery is for both. So long as it is remembered separately, whether in pride or in humiliation, it constitutes perhaps the most deeply divisive factor in the tragic conflict, because no merely current interest could unite each group vis-a-vis the other at so deep a level. But, by the same token, when the time comes, as surely it will—indeed, it is beginning to come even now—when the two groups will remember slavery together, in mutual understanding and acceptance, then there will come to pass in the South a deeper community between white and black than could possibly be known elsewhere in the nation.

The common memories which lie deep in the existence of a great people cannot be carefully measured or defined. Who will distinguish, or separate out, the strands of memory which bind the generations together in England or China or France? Obviously, no one can. But the indefiniteness of these memories must not lead us into the positivistic error of denying their existence and their importance. When Lincoln in the final sentence of his First Inaugural Address predicted that "the mystic chords of memory stretching from every battle field and patriot grave to every living heart and hearthstone over this broad land, will yet swell the chorus of Union when again touched, as surely they will be, by the better angels of our nature," he was not being either sentimental or fanciful, but was appealing to the deepest element in the actual unity of the nation. No military victory or political rearrangement could so firmly have united a people whose memories were not shared.

Before leaving the subject of community memory in general and turning more specifically to the Church, it may be well to raise the question of its historical value. Does it yield any reliable knowledge of the past? Does it have any significance for the historian? Certainly we shall not expect him to make any but the most cautious use of it. His judgments about the past are normally based on documents or other tangible records, and he is bound to be skeptical about any "remembered" fact which documents do not confirm. This is as it ought to be. The kind of memory we have been considering is not, for the most part, concerned with facts in the ordinary sense and is certainly not good at preserving them clearly or accurately. Even individuals do not remember names and dates very well; communities can hardly be said to remember them at all. But the significance of communal memory lies, not in its accuracy in such matters, but in its effectiveness in preserving something of the concrete quality, the felt meaning, of an event in the past; and here, it seems to me, one cannot deny to it all objective historical value. The actual impact of the Civil War's end and aftermath upon the South was almost certainly not unlike what I "remember" it to have been. To be sure, this impact is described or revealed in so many contemporary documents that the historian does not need to rely on any remembrance of mine. But if literary source materials were lacking and he decided to trust the memory of my generation in the South, he would not in actual fact be mistaken in concluding both that the war and its sequel of confusion and suffering occurred and that it had the concrete meanings for the people of the South, both white and black, of which "living" memory would have made him aware.

For the purposes of this argument, the value of communal memories for scientific historiography does not need to be demonstrated, either as fact or as possibility. Our main point is, not that they are true, but that they exist—that is, exist as memories. Their content is for those who hold them a *remembered* content and therefore is *for them* not only true as facts are true, but real as actual life is real—the one, because the other. To share in a common memory is to participate in an experience of the meaning of a past event whose actuality can be as little doubted as the meaning itself.

If in this there be any truth at all, it cannot seem strange that one should speak of the Church's "memory" and more particularly of its memory of Jesus. Whatever else the Church is, it is a historical community, a cultural stream flowing without interruption from the first century into our own. Not merely its outward forms of belief and cult, but its inner substance has been largely transmitted from generation to generation in a continuous corporate life. Of this inner substance, as in all historical communities, shared memories form a large part; and that among these there should be some memory of Jesus himself ought not to seem incredible. So much can be said simply on the basis of the Church's nature as a historical community; but when one considers certain unique characteristics of the Church—features which distinguish it from other historical communities and make it the particular community it is—one finds that all we have observed about the reality and importance of common memory in the existence of historical communities acquires new point and force.

The first of these unique features appears when we remind ourselves of the singular significance which history has for the Church. Any work on modern historiography[1] is likely to note this fact and its importance. The Church has always been uniquely preoccupied with the idea of history, and it is hardly too much to say that it was in its life and thought that history first acquired full reality and universality. By "reality" I mean real movement in real time, from a beginning in the past to an end in the future—not the interminable cycle of nature, nor yet the mere successive bodying forth in transient

[1] As, e.g., that of R. G. Collingwood, *The Idea of History* (Oxford: Clarendon Press, 1946), pp. 46-52. The quoted phrase later in this paragraph is taken from this passage.

forms of eternal and unchanging ideas. History involved real change; its events were not appearances only, "flowing, so to speak, over the surfaces of things," but were of the stuff and substance of existence. God was not aloof and inert; he was an actor, a doer. There was a *time* when he made the world out of nothing and there will be a *time* when he will bring it to an end. Meanwhile, he is working in it, creating and destroying, judging and healing.

This way of realizing the meaning of history had long been characteristic of Hebrew thought; but in being appropriated by the Church it was set free from nationalistic presuppositions which had limited and to a degree corrupted it. All mankind in the whole range of its history was now seen to constitute the field of God's creative work. The Church was no favored class or race, static and closed. It was created to be the constantly enlarging sphere of God's healing, reconciling action for and among all men; and the center of universal history was the moment when this "creation" took place, this "action" began. Unless it be the Hebrew-Jewish people, no historical community has ever been so fully engaged with history, so deeply involved in it and so profoundly aware of its own involvement, as the Christian Church. And unless it be the Exodus from Egypt, no historical event has ever been the object of such constant recall and such sustained reflection as the Event in which the Church had its rise. Would we not expect that in such a community memory would have an especially large place?

We must note, as a second feature, how completely dominated the remembered Event is by the person of Jesus. I have referred to the Event as the coming into existence of the Church. This, I have argued in the preceding chapter, is the only accurate and adequate way formally to define the Event, and most of this book will be devoted to showing the important implications of this formal definition. But it says nothing about the actual content of the Event—persons, circumstances, incidents—the "material," so to speak, to which the Church's beginning gave unity, meaning, and identity. Now I should say that all *evaluation* of the Event, all *theological interpretation* of it, will have its ground, whether recognized or not, in one's acceptance of the truth of the formal definition I have proposed. But it is equally clear that whatever *memory* we may have of the Event must be memory of its "content." One does not "remember" ideas or concepts or generalizations or formal definitions, however true they may be; one *remembers* only persons and things and happenings. And of this remembered content of the so-called Christ Event, Jesus is the completely dominating center. Is there another important event in human history consisting to so large an extent in the simple existence of a single individual and the response which he awakened? Surely we may say, then, that if in the Christian community there has come down within and through the generations any authentic memory of its beginnings, that memory is a memory of him.

We may observe, in passing, that this central and dominating position of Jesus and his career within the content of the Event makes somewhat difficult and strange for us the definition of its essential character which I have been defending. I feel sure we find it easier to agree with the definition of the American Revolution as the coming into being of the United States of America than with the corresponding definition of the Event of Christ as the coming into being of the Church. And I suggest that the greater difficulty in the latter case is associated with the comparative simplicity of the content of the Event. When we consider the Revolution in its actual progress, we are concerned with declarations from many sources, battles won and lost by many warriors, decisions made and executed by many statesmen. In a word, we see a complicated interplay of persons and other factors; and, looking for unity, we are almost driven to recognize in the *issue* of the contest, in the emergence of the independent state, the only clue to its meaning and therefore to its being as the particular historical event it was. But although it is just as true that the Event of Christ has its reality as such in the emergence of the Church, this fact is more likely to be hidden from us because of the relative simplicity of what we actually see. Because Jesus is so incomparably important in the content of the Event, we find it easy to suppose that we do not need to look further than his career for its meaning. But this supposition is mistaken. Nothing could be more surely true than that the man Jesus—what he was heard to say and seen to do, what he was known to be, what was observed to happen to him—was the supremely important, almost the sole, content of the Event; for this reason we remember him. But it is not this remembered or recorded content which makes the Event the particular event it was, but rather the emerging community, where alone the memory had existence and Jesus himself historical importance.

A third feature of the Church which has the effect of establishing in a unique way the memory of Jesus within its life is its knowledge of the Resurrection. The meaning of this knowledge requires a chapter of its own, but its relation to the Church's memory must at least be noted now, although this aspect of the general theme will also belong within the later discussion. Not infrequently the "risen Christ" has been set rather sharply over against the "Jesus of history." If by the latter phrase one means the "Jesus" whose existence and character can be established by the methods of the historian, the separation is perhaps justified, for this "Jesus" may be found outside the Church, whereas the "risen Christ" can be known only within it. But if by the "Jesus of history" one means simply the man of Nazareth, the human Jesus, then the kind of separation we often make between the terms is not legitimate, for the particular knowledge of this Jesus which the Church has and treasures, quite as truly as its knowledge of the risen Lord, can be found only within it. He is *remembered* there; and the very meaning of the term "resurrection" requires the prior existence of this memory. The Church could not recognize one whom it did not remember. We cannot know again what we have not known before. The knowledge of Christ risen from the dead not only is inalienable, but also is near the center of the Church's existence. The meaning of that statement we shall consider more fully later. The point just now is that this knowledge inescapably and constantly implies the remembrance of Jesus, and that every recognition of Christ's reality and living presence in the worship of the Church is also an appeal to a memory of the human Jesus which belongs just as essentially to the Church's life.

This reference to worship suggests the last two items in this review of unique features of the Church. One of these is the customary reading from the New Testament, the collection of documents produced by the Church under the immediate impact of the Event and reflecting most vividly the primitive remembrance of Jesus. Here we are bound to think, first of all, of the Gospels, but the Epistles are almost as important, and sometimes even more important. For although the Epistles are less concerned with the facts of Jesus' career, they reflect, often more directly and immediately than the Gospels, the Church's remembrance of the man himself. The more precise relation of these early documents, especially the Gospels, to the Church's memory will be discussed a little later; but that the constant devotional use of them in private and corporate worship since very early times has had the effect of emphasizing within the life of the Church the importance of its memory of Jesus and of confirming the memory itself —this is so obvious as to need no discussion.

The final item, and certainly one of the most important, is the Lord's Supper. This rite has been the central act in the worship of the Church since the very beginning. It probably antedates both Scripture reading and preaching in Christian worship, although the associations of the three are very early and very close. The Supper has many meanings, symbolizing as it does the whole concrete reality of the Church's existence and of our actual, almost bodily, participation in it, and it will be referred to in other connections. Of particular relevance just now is the fact that the Supper has always been in a pre-eminent sense an occasion for recalling Jesus. It has always been "in remembrance of [him]." Long before the Gospels were written or before what Justin Martyr called "the memoirs of the apostles" could be read, Christians were asking, "Do you remember . . . ?" or were exhorting one another to "remember," as they met in their weekly or daily celebrations of God's creative, saving act in Christ—an act in the very substance of which they were being given to share. Ought it to be surprising that such a historical community, at the center of whose corporate life from its beginning had been such an act of remembrance, should have preserved some authentic memory of Jesus?

But whether deemed "authentic" or not by the disinterested observer, the memory is bound to seem so to one who shares in it; and this is the principal point I am seeking to make. The image the Church has of Jesus is such an image as belongs to memory. As such it is the Church's intimate and sure possession.

Thus far in this chapter we have dealt only with the question whether we can properly speak of the Church's "remembering" at all and, more particularly, of its "remembering" Jesus. We must now consider what this memory contains and how it is related to the Gospels, our only written records of Jesus' life. These two questions are closely related and can be best discussed together.

We may begin with a remark which applies not only to the Gospels, but also to the New Testament in all its parts. These documents are more valuable for the testimony they bear to the existence and nature of the early Church's memory of Jesus than for any statement of more "objective" fact they may make about him and his career. This is true because of both the greater certainty of this testimony and its greater relevance. As regards certainty, it is clear that the ancient documents put us directly and indubitably in touch with the memory, whereas we must establish the more objective facts by inference and argument. In many cases this can be done with the highest degree of probability; still, it remains true that any knowledge derived from the New Testament of what, precisely, Jesus said or did is, and must be, less certain than the knowledge of how he was remembered to have spoken and acted, and that any knowledge derived from this same source of what he was is really knowledge of what he was remembered as being. But the latter kind of knowledge has also the greater relevance. For Jesus of Nazareth, Jesus as a human being, insofar as he has any importance for Christian existence, is a memory of the Church. We will not say "only a memory," any more than a devoted family will say "only a memory" in referring to a deceased parent. In both cases the person in the past is very real and very important; but he exists as someone remembered, however significant the memory may be. One way of describing the Church is to say that it is the community which remembers Jesus; but one can equally truly define Jesus (in the only really significant meaning of that name for the Christian) as the one who is remembered. It is only as he is remembered that he has meaning for either Christian theology or Christian devotion. In a word, the human existence of Jesus, insofar as it has continuing being and importance, is a memory of the Church.

Although the reminder is probably not necessary, it will be safer to point out that we cannot think of the New Testament as providing us with an extra-ecclesiastical source for the "historical Jesus," or indeed for anything else. If the only surviving memory of Jesus is the Church's memory, the New Testament, which attempts (among other things) to record and convey that memory, is even more obviously the Church's book. Its several documents were written out of the Church's experience, and out of that experience alone. It does not provide us with a place to stand outside the Church; on the contrary, it draws us more deeply into the Church. It does not bring us what happened in some purely objective sense (as though that would be possible anyhow), but what was believed, and often remembered, to have happened by those among whom the event first occurred. To be sure, the New Testament does serve as a check upon, as well as a resource for, the life of the Church (including its memory) in every age, but this is because it speaks to us directly out of the life of the Church and the memory of the Church in its first, and in some ways most authentic, age—not because it has a position outside the Church or even alongside the Church in any sense or degree whatever. Its experience of Christ is in every respect the Church's experience; its memory of Jesus, the Church's memory.

When we ask more precisely how the memory of the Church is related to what the Gospels say, I believe one must answer that the Church remembers both more and less than the Gospels contain. It remembers *more* inasmuch as its image of Jesus himself, especially in his relation to his disciples, is not fully provided by the Gospels and could not be derived from them. It remembers *less* inasmuch as most of the factual content of such knowledge of Jesus as we have is provided by the Gospels alone. Since the second of these statements is likely to appear the more obviously true, we shall consider it first.

Here I must make clear that in affirming that a memory of Jesus exists in the Church, I am not suggesting that it contains a single specific datum concerning the circumstances or incidents of Jesus' career or a single sentence from his lips—that it contains anything at all which might in a specific way confirm, discredit, correct or supplement any item in the Gospels. For such facts of Jesus' career we are entirely dependent upon the written sources—and, one may add, upon these sources as understood by the critical historian. When I say, then, that the Church remembers Jesus, I do not mean that it remembers *facts about him*. Indeed, it is doubtful that we can ever properly be said to *remember* a fact about anything. Facts about things are abstractions; only the things themselves can in the strict sense be remembered. Although it would be rash indeed to say that many of the facts stated in the Gospels—that Jesus said or did this or that, that he went here or there, that this or that thing happened to him or in his presence—do not go back to a primitive memory of concrete events themselves, it would be much more rash to assert that there has persisted in the Church any independent remembrance of these same facts by which they can be tested. I certainly do not want to be understood as making such an assertion. The Gospels obviously tell us more about Jesus than any "memory" of the Church can be said to contain.

Moreover, they tell us a great deal. We have recognized the character of the Gospels as "Church books," reflecting in manifold ways the experiences and reflections of the churches in the final decades of the first century and adapted to meeting the felt needs of these primitive communities. But undoubtedly one of these felt needs was the need of authentic information about Jesus; and equally certainly the basic material in the composition of the Gospels was a tradition about him which went back to the earliest memories of the Church. Discrimination between this basic material and later accretions is exceedingly difficult and can never perhaps be at the same time both precise and sure. But I stand with those who believe that however critical our methods may be, we are left with a very substantial residuum of historically trustworthy fact about Jesus, his teaching and his life. It would fall outside the purpose of this book to try to indicate either the contents or the limits of this body of information;[2] but it is, without any question, considerable; and new studies in fresh areas (as, for example, in the Dead Sea Scrolls) are to a degree clarifying and confirming it. Although one could not

[2] The recently translated book of G. Bornkamm, *Jesus of Nazareth* (New York: Harper & Brothers, 1961) is of great significance because of its success in doing this.

truly say that the Church vitally requires this information—
the Church really needs to know of Jesus only what it "remembers" of him—nevertheless, it is of great importance to
the Church and we can be immensely grateful for it. My
point at the moment, however, is simply that the Gospels
undoubtedly tell us more about Jesus than any independent
memory of the Church could conceivably provide.

But they also tell us less—and here a longer argument will
be required. They tell us less because the image of Jesus himself which the Church carries in its heart cannot be derived
simply and solely from the Gospels and has not in fact been
derived from that source. It existed before the Gospels were
written, and the Gospels, when they were written, did not
displace it. The Gospels performed the immense service of
putting into written form the words of Jesus and the stories
about him with which the earliest shared memories of Jesus
were associated. They do for us what the original materials
of this kind, orally repeated in teaching and worship, did
for the primitive Church. Not only would the remembrance
of Jesus be immeasurably poorer without them; it is hard to
see how, without them, it could ever have existed at all in any
tangible or communicable form. But to say this is not to say
that the memory itself was in early times nothing more than
the aggregate of the scattered oral traditions and that now it is
simply the Gospels which contain them. Such a statement is
not true to the facts of the Church's life.

For the truth of the matter is that, whether the Church
is deemed to have a right to this knowledge or not, it has
always known more of Jesus than the Gospels tell us—not,
I repeat, more facts about him or his life, but more of the man
himself. Its picture of Jesus has not been derived solely
from the Gospels. One can almost hear the obvious ironical
retort: "Of course not! But how much better if it had been!
Every generation and class of Christians has had its own
picture. Each age has constructed 'Jesus' in its own image."
The truth in this charge is not to be denied; the "peril of

modernizing Jesus" is always present and is never entirely escaped. But having recognized this, we must not make the opposite error of assuming that all we truly know about the Jesus of the past is written in the Gospels and that therefore everything in the Church's image of Jesus which cannot be derived from a critical examination of the Gospels is an example of modernizing fancy. Such a conclusion denies the possibility that there has come down within the body of the Church—in, around, and underneath the Gospel materials and reflected more directly in certain statements in the Epistles —an authentic remembrance of Jesus. This a priori denial is arbitrary and ignores a basic element in the existence of all historical communities and of the Church in particular: the persistence of memory, the continuing presence, however muted, of what Papias centuries ago in this same connection called "the living and abiding voice."[3]

I venture to suggest two elements in this memory. One of them has to do with the personal moral stature of Jesus. This, I believe the Church knows, was greater than the Gospels alone would force us to conclude. Let it not be thought that I am in the slightest degree disparaging the greatness of the person who would emerge simply from the Gospels; I *am* saying that this person is not so great as the Church "remembers" Jesus to have been. The proof of this lies in the fact that critical studies of the "life" of Jesus, even when written by the ablest and most responsible historians on the basis of the most honest and careful examination of the

[3] Quoted in Eusebius, *Church History*, III. 39. 4.
This "memory" is obviously related to what the Church has called "tradition," but is not to be identified with it. The "memory," unlike "tradition," does not contain either factual data in the ordinary sense or doctrinal formulations. Its content is more concrete. So far as the original Event is concerned, it is only Jesus himself who is *remembered*. Still, it seems to me that a sound instinct has been at work among those who have insisted on the reality and importance of an extrascriptural source of knowledge of the Church's own intimate past. On this general subject see G. H. Tavard, *Holy Writ or Holy Church* (New York: Harper & Brothers, 1959), especially the discussion of John Eck on pp. 117 ff.

Gospels, have never succeeded in satisfying the Church—that is, in seeming really adequate and true. I do not think that one can explain this fact by saying: "The historians have not been sufficiently gifted. They have lacked imagination and insight. The Gospels really say more about the 'historical Jesus' than historians have been able or have taken the trouble to hear." Such a statement would be unfair to scholars like Goguel and Guinebert, Case and Cadbury.[4] But neither can one explain the Church's dissatisfaction with such critical studies by saying: "The Church has in its mind the image of a divine being whom the historian cannot find in history simply because he was never there, and in the nature of the case, could never have been there. It has created out of its later experiences and reflection a purely illusory image of Jesus and can be content with nothing else." Such a statement does not do justice to the Church's concern for truth. Although both "explanations" are valid and relevant up to a certain point, they fall short of fully explaining the biographer's "failure." What must also be taken into account is the fact that we are dealing here, not with a historical figure known only through documentary sources, but with a beloved person the memory of whom has come down from generation to generation within the body of an organic human community. The fact that this process of transmission would probably have been quite impossible without the Gospels to guide and guard it must not blind us to the fact that it is something more and other than the Gospels. The Church has an impression of the moral greatness of Jesus which cannot have been derived simply from these books. Indeed, are we not constantly reading them, and sometimes even correcting them, under

4 I have in mind such books as M. Goguel, *The Life of Jesus,* trans. O. Wyon (New York: The Macmillan Company, 1933); C. A. H. Guignebert, *Jesus,* trans. S. H. Hooke (London: Kegan Paul, Trench, Trubner & Co., 1935); S. J. Case, *Jesus; a New Biography* (Chicago: University of Chicago Press, 1927); H. J. Cadbury, *The Peril of Modernizing Jesus* (New York: The Macmillan Company, 1937); *Jesus: What Manner of Man?* (New York: The Macmillan Company, 1947).

the influence of this prior impression? Here, as I have already hinted, the Epistles may often be more important than the Gospels because they reflect it more immediately.

The Christian cannot regard this impression as illusory, and one may offer strong arguments for its truth by appealing to the magnitude of the historical consequences which followed upon the brief career. But the Church's impression does not rest upon such arguments, nor can it be fully justified or sustained by them. One must simply say that the impression is there, that it belongs, and has always belonged, to the existence of the Church. It is a feature of what can only be called the Church's remembrance of Jesus. Others may doubt its truth; the Church is incapable of doing so.

Another element in the Church's image of Jesus which does not rest solely on what the Gospels say has to do with the relation in which he stood to his disciples and friends, and they to him. The relation was from the beginning remembered as one of love, that same kind or quality of love (agape) which the Church now knew as the bond of unity within its own life. It not only *knew* this love as a present continuing reality within the fellowship of the Church, but it also *remembered* it as already manifested in Jesus. Here again we touch on the meaning of the Resurrection, for the agape known in the Church, and known there as the Spirit of God, his very presence, could not have been recognized also as the Spirit of Christ if the same agape had not been remembered as the essential and distinctive quality of Jesus' own life.

I have said that the Church's knowledge of this quality goes beyond what the Gospels say. These are, generally speaking, strangely silent about Jesus' own inner attitudes, states of mind and heart. They tell us where he went, what he did or said, what happened to him, but rarely give us any hint of what he was feeling. One may infer from his teaching about God how he himself felt toward God, but we are not explicitly told. One may draw conclusions from his ethical teaching, not only as to how he *thought* about one's duty toward others, but also as to what his actual feelings toward others were; but these are never described and are seldom referred to. Sometimes, in his most passionate (and most characteristic) teachings, his inner feelings break through what may appear to be the determined objectivity of the Gospel record, and one seems for a moment to hear his very voice. But these occasions are rare indeed; and I wonder just what impression of the inner personal life of Jesus we should have if we needed to depend on the Gospels alone, or whether we should be able to hear his voice in his recorded words if we were not also hearing it in the common life of the Church.

My point, however, is somewhat different from this. I am referring primarily, not to the characteristic attitudes of Jesus toward God and toward men generally, but to his more intimate relation with those who responded to him and who formed the company of his disciples; and here, I believe it is true to say, the "memory" of the Church goes far beyond anything a critical reading of the Gospels would alone justify. Undoubtedly one reason the Church has always cherished the Fourth Gospel and has been unable to believe that it does not contain authentic historical truth about Jesus is that one can read there, and there only, such words as "Having loved his own . . . he loved them to the end" and "This is my commandment, that you love one another as I have loved you" (John 13:1; 15:12)—words which express a love of Jesus for his own which has a deep, sure place in the memory of the Church. Here again this memory is first reflected in the Epistles: when Paul speaks of "the love of Christ," he is "remembering" the love of Jesus for his disciples as well as recognizing the gracious presence of the risen Lord. But it is only *reflected* there. It existed already in the body of the Church and exists there still, deeply indebted to Gospels and Epistles, but not created by them, not exhausted by them, and never entirely to be displaced by them.

In all of this I have not been trying to establish data which the secular historian will find acceptable or usable in his attempt to construct "the historical Jesus." Indeed, I can readily believe that many a *Christian* historian will turn from this chapter, not only unconvinced that we can properly speak of the Church's memory of Jesus, but also persuaded that to do so is to be sentimental, if not dangerously obscurantist. To the latter I would only say: "Examine yourself. Is the image of the human Jesus which you possess as a Christian derived entirely from the facts established by the Gospels, and are you no more certain of it than this evidence justifies? Is not your image of Jesus both richer and surer than this? I believe it is. Either, then, you divide yourself: as a Christian affirming what as a historian you know you have no right to affirm; or you are mistaken in thinking that you do not share in, depend on, and trust as valid and true, the Church's memory of Jesus." This memory is one aspect of the existential reality of the Church. Whatever evaluation may be made of it by others, the Church's picture of Jesus has what seems to it to be the character of a remembrance—that is, it is the picture of someone known to have been real. And this remembrance is absolutely vital to its existence. It is this fact about the Church—or, better, it is this element in its nature—which makes impossible its accepting any denial of the existence of Jesus or any disparagement of his importance. What God did in bringing the new community into being was done, it knows, through him.

Because our primary concern up to this point in this book has been with the kind of present being the human Jesus may be said to have, our treatment of the Church's memory has been largely limited to its significance as the locus of that being. For the sake of the total purpose of this book, however, it may be well, before closing this chapter, to make two points about the memory which have been more than once implied, but on which no special emphasis has thus far been laid. One of these is its importance (we are speaking now, not of the remembrance of Jesus only, but of memory in a broader, more inclusive sense) as an element in the substance, the integrity and the unity of the Church. I spoke earlier of the memories, never to be fully plumbed or carefully measured, which belong to the inner existence of a great nation. Deep springs of common memory both nourish its life and largely determine its distinctive character. But for the Church these springs are deeper, welling up directly and continuously from a more ancient past and from profounder levels of conscious and subconscious association and loyalty, than can be true for any nation. Judaism alone would provide a comparable case. The remembrance of Jesus, of whom we have been principally speaking, is the central element in a whole complex of remembrances, comprising what H. Richard Niebuhr in an eloquent passage calls "the internal history" of the Church.[5] Just as my own memories of the past, my "internal history," make up no small part of the substance of my personal existence, so the concrete being of the Church, not only depends on a common remembering of the past, but, to a large degree, actually consists in the substance of these memories. Its "body" is in large part a body of remembrances. No wonder Scripture, tradition, and ancient liturgical practice are significant to it! These are the symbols, and therefore the bearers, of its "inner history," of the concrete content of its memory. But they are important only because the memory itself is more important still. This memory, woven into the warp and woof of the Church's existence, belongs to it ineradicably and is one of the basic elements in both its distinctiveness and its unity. The garment may have been torn out of shape or even rent apart, but the fabric, with its characteristic texture, is still the same.

The second point is the consideration that the kind of appropriation of the past about which we have been speaking

[5] *The Meaning of Revelation* (New York: The Macmillan Company, 1941), pp. 43 ff.

as characteristic of the Church makes the past in a real sense not past at all, but a dimension, so to speak, of a present existence. Just as what I remember of my own past belongs to my present being, so the memory of the Church has the effect of binding the generations and the centuries into one present time. The saints and martyrs, the reformers and prophets, the Fathers and Apostles, belong to this ampler "present" of the Church's existence. Only what antedates, or in some other way is external to, this "time" of the Church must be relegated wholly and solely to the past and therefore placed beyond our grasp. The main contention of these two chapters has been that Jesus himself belongs, not to this inaccessible "past," but, as one remembered, to the present existence of the living Church.

III *The Church and the Resurrection*

I HAVE SAID THAT THE CHURCH COULD NOT, WITHOUT CEASING to be the Church, conclude, or even consider the possibility, that Jesus never lived, that he whom it "remembers" did not exist at all. The same impossibility of denying a past fact can be affirmed equally confidently at one other point, and, I believe, at only one other point: the Church, without ceasing or having ceased to be the Church, could not deny, or even doubt, that God raised Jesus from the dead.

It is important to note that the grounds for the Church's assertions in both cases lie in its own life. The assertion of Jesus' existence rests, we have seen, in its memory. It would be palpably false to say that the Church knows that Jesus existed because the historians have assured it that he did. The truth of the matter is, rather, that the principal argument the historians have for his existence is the Church's prior knowledge of it—that is, a memory of Jesus which can be traced back continuously through the centuries to the time when the Church first emerged into consciousness of itself. How, they ask, can this memory be explained if Jesus did not live? But the Church, which has the memory, does not need the argument. Its own existence being, so to speak, the major premise, it does not need to wait for the conclusion. It may find the argument useful for apologetic purposes, but it is not in the position of having to depend on it for its own assurance. The Church's assurance that Jesus lived is not a rational inference from its existence, but belongs to the existence itself. A demonstration that he did not live is, from the Church's point of view, impossible and unthinkable, just as a demonstration that the persons I remember as my father and mother did not live would be from mine. If in the latter case such a demonstration should actually be accomplished, far more would be involved for me than the necessity of revising my opinion of the past or adjusting myself to a new idea; it is not too much to say that my own existence as the person I am would be, or would have been, destroyed. I should no longer be myself. I do not believe we truly see the relation in which the Church stands to the fact of Jesus until we recognize that the memory of the man and the existence of the community are related to each other in the same essential and inextricable way. This was the theme of the preceding chapter. The point just now is that the community's assurance of the Resurrection—by which at the moment I mean, simply and plainly, its assurance that Jesus was alive after his death —belongs just as surely, as intimately, and as essentially to the being of the Church.

This is true because the Christian community was from the beginning a sharing, not only in a common memory of Jesus, but also in a common experience of the Spirit—the Spirit being experienced as the Spirit of God, the Creator of the heavens and the earth, the Lord of all nature and history, and also as the personal reality, the very being and presence, of the same Jesus who was remembered. In this fact —that the Spirit was experienced, and was *thus* experienced, within the Church—we have the whole explanation of the Resurrection faith as well as of every other distinctive and essential character or element in its life. If this fact is affirmed, everything is affirmed; if it is denied, the whole Christian position not only becomes untenable, but simply disappears.

The fact is threefold, and each part of it needs to be emphasized. First, it must be insisted that when one speaks of the Spirit, one is speaking of something in *experience,* of something known or knowable in the immediate way we know ourselves and other persons and the concrete things about us. One is referring, not primarily to a conception or to the object of a conception, but to a felt reality. Just as the Church actually remembered Jesus, so it actually experienced the Spirit. Thus, the Spirit in the New Testament is sometimes spoken of as a tangible, even material, thing—the Spirit is "poured out," "received," it "fills"; sometimes, as a personal being—"coming," "speaking," "possessing"; but always as an actual entity, an object of concrete knowledge.

In our ordinary use, the word "spirit" has a rather different sense. It refers to a quality of a person or group or occasion —a characteristic attitude or feeling tone. We speak of one's having a "friendly spirit," meaning no more than that one is friendly, or of a group as having a "co-operative spirit," when we mean simply that the members are mutually helpful. We may speak of the "spirit" of a meeting as being "good" when relations among persons and parties are cordial and a common purpose is supported with some unanimity and enthusiasm. In other words, the term "spirit" is for us often a psychological term designating the attitude of an individual or group, whether occasional or habitual.

But is there a single instance of this understanding of "spirit" in the New Testament, or, for that matter, in the Bible as a whole? What we know concerning ancient, and particularly Jewish, thinking about psychology, with the emphasis upon the concrete and the material, would hardly lead us to expect it; and as a matter of fact I am doubtful that we find it. It has been argued that we have an instance of this usage in Rom. 8:15, which is rendered in the Revised Standard Version: "For you did not receive the spirit of slavery to fall back into fear, but you have received the spirit of sonship"; but I am sure that the New English Bible is at this point more accurate: "The Spirit you have received is not a spirit of slavery leading you back into a life of fear but a Spirit that makes us sons." Nor must we be deceived by the lowercase "spirit of slavery" in the latter sentence into supposing that the meaning is simply "a slavish attitude." Undoubtedly Paul means to be saying: "The Spirit you have received does not make slaves of you, but rather sons."

So throughout the New Testament "spirit" means, not a quality or disposition, but an actual personal reality. The word may refer to the "spirit" of a man, his psyche or self. The reference may be to an "evil spirit," a demonic personal power. Or it may be to the Spirit of God, the Holy Spirit— that is, to God himself, present and active, to the very reality of his own divine being, become manifest and immanent. The word is much more often employed in the last of these senses than in either of the other two, and the term "the Spirit" is always thus used. The Spirit is the Holy Spirit of God, who brooded over the face of the waters at Creation, who moves in all nature and history, who called, and spoke through, the prophets, who enlightened and comforted the psalmists and all the saints of Israel. When the Spirit is being identified with God himself, he is spoken of in fully personal terms; when the identification is rather with God's "presence" or his "power," less personal words and images are employed; but always God's own reality is being referred to, and always this reality is making itself known or felt in a tangible or concrete way, whether in nature or among men.

There is a new element, however, in the concrete meaning of the term as it was used within the Christian community. The Spirit is known also as "the Spirit of Christ" or "the Spirit of Jesus." I say "concrete meaning," for the situation was not that the Church merely *conceived* of the Spirit in this way, but that it actually received or experienced the Spirit so. The Spirit it knew, the Spirit in which it was by definition a sharing, the Spirit whose presence and power were felt in the fellowship—this Spirit made itself indubitably known, not only as the Spirit of God, but also, and in a way which defied logic or any kind of explanation, as Jesus' own Spirit: the personal reality of him whom his disciples *remembered* together they were now *experiencing* together as a present fact. The Spirit meant not only the actual presence in their midst of the transcendent God to whom they looked up in worship, but, equally inexplicably, the actual presence of the Jesus to whom they looked back in remembrance.

It will be easy to say that this immediate awareness of the actual presence of Christ in the worship of the Church and in its common life is an illusion, and that the "experience" referred to is simply the result of the suggestive power of an idea. The remembrance of Jesus was so vivid that, along with other psychological and historical factors, it led to the "experience" of his "presence." The *thought* of him was present; his "spirit" (in the sense of his remembered attitudes and mental and moral traits) was present; and only in this sense was *he* ever present or is he present still. I have no intention of trying to refute such an argument. I do not believe the argument can be refuted, any more than the argument of the solipsist can be refuted. All I am concerned to say is that the Church could not possibly be convinced of its truth. Just as it could not be persuaded that it does not remember Jesus, so it could not be persuaded that it does not know him still. In the breaking of bread and in prayer it both remembers him and knows his living presence. Christian community is by definition a sharing in this memory and in this presence.

The Church in its essential and distinctive nature is the historical body in which this memory of the human Jesus and this experience of him as the divine Lord are fused or welded into an indivisible whole. One cannot remember Jesus (as the Church remembers him) without realizing that one also knows him now as Lord and Christ; but one cannot so know him without also remembering him as man and Master. The two kinds of experience, so inextricably mingled, are not without effect upon each other. Undoubtedly our present knowledge of Jesus is decisively affected by our memory of him; and it is probably just as true that our memory of him has to some extent been shaped by our knowledge of his present reality. But the memory cannot be "explained" as a mere projection backward of the Church's later experience any more than the experience can be "explained" as the mere effect of reflection on the memory. Nor is the fusion of the two so complete as to obliterate the distinction between them. The Cross unmistakably and inerasably marks the decisive break. But the break is between elements whose continuity and involvement with each other just as surely and clearly confront us in the present concrete reality of Jesus Christ our Lord.

It is interesting to observe this duality in the symbolic significance and, to a degree, in the liturgy of the Lord's Supper. There is some evidence for the view that in the earliest Church the rite had two forms: one finding its type in Jesus' last meal with his disciples before his death; and the other, in the meals at which he was present with them after his Resurrection (Luke 24:30, 36; John 12:12; Acts 1:4 [mg.]).[1] For some Christians, then (according to this view), the Supper was primarily "in remembrance of him" and especially of "his death and passion" and might even be thought of as a sharing in his sacrifice; for others, it was a joyous celebration of the Resurrection, a glad acknowledgment of his living reality, and an act of communion with him as living Spirit. Whatever one's judgment of this view may be, it is easy to understand that the Supper may at some place and time have had each of these meanings because it was so clearly inevitable that in its full development it should have both. If it was to be the central act of the Church's worship, it *had* to embody a recognition of the two elements in the Church's essential nature—the devoted remembrance of Jesus and the joyous knowledge of the risen Christ.

[1] See H. Lietzmann, *Messe und Herrenmahl* (Bonn: Marcus & Weber, 1926) and O. Cullmann, *Early Christian Worship* (London: SCM Press, 1953), pp. 14-20. There are significant differences between the two writers.

The Resurrection is our way of referring to these two elements in the Church's existence in their relation to each other and to whatever must be presupposed when we think of them. It is hard to see how we can speak of them at all without saying something like: "This Jesus . . . crucified and killed . . . God raised up" (Acts 2:23-24). But this affirmation of a past event is at its base an affirmation of a present reality— namely, the realized identity of the one remembered with the one known. The present reality does not exist because the past event is affirmed; rather, the past event is affirmed because the present reality exists. To share in the substance of the Church's life is to know the concrete meaning of the Resurrection. To affirm the Resurrection is to affirm the distinctive character of the Church's own existence.

This being true, the Church does not need to argue for the Resurrection, and indeed places itself in a position of great weakness when it tries. We have seen that no argument for the fact of Jesus—that is, of the Jesus the Church remembers—can be adequate; it is much more obvious that one cannot demonstrate by evidence and argument the fact of the Resurrection. Outside the Church, the evidence cannot be seen; inside the Church, the argument is not needed. It is not surprising that the Church, both under the goadings of the hostile critic and in seeking to persuade the honest skeptic, should have resorted to argument. Paul, for example, troubled by what he understands to be the doubts of the Resurrection of Christ among the Christians at Corinth, seeks to silence them with an account, the earliest that has come down to us, of the visual experiences of the risen Jesus had by his disciples. The weakness of the argument appears in the clearly implied admission that although Paul hopes these data will convince the Corinthians, they had not convinced *him*. Indeed, although he had heard all the "evidence," he was a zealous persecutor of the Church and called the Resurrection preaching blasphemy until, "last of all," Jesus appeared also to him. In other words, he was not persuaded of the Resurrection by hearsay testimony although he seems to be supposing here that others may be.

Actually no one could be persuaded of it thus. The Resurrection is not such a fact as can be thus proved. Either one does not need the evidence or one finds it woefully inadequate. Either one is sure before the argument starts or one is even more skeptical after it ends. Visions, even if acknowledged to have happened, can be dreams or hallucinations, the products of overstimulated imaginations or of morbid desires or fears. The finding of an empty tomb, even if admitted, can be more plausibly explained by a mistake on someone's part as to where the body was buried or by someone's having removed the body from its original place, than by a "resurrection." These "evidences" are weak and futile, possibly credible only to those who do not need them. I do not mean that visual experiences of the risen Jesus did not occur, but, rather, that such "signs" can be "infallible" only to those who actually receive them. Nor am I denying that in the Providence of God these experiences served to open the way to that knowledge of the actual living reality of God in Christ which was the only effective ground of the Resurrection faith, whether among the few who had had the experiences or among the multitudes who had not. For all of these, the valid evidence of Jesus' Resurrection was the realized presence and power of the Christ they remembered, alive after his passion. This evidence was provided only within the Church's existence. To share in that existence is, for us also, to "know him and the power of his resurrection" and thus to possess the only possible reason for believing in the Resurrection at all. And as for those outside, they will come to know the meaning of the Resurrection of Christ and to believe its truth only when, despite the feebleness of our witness to our living Lord, they are drawn (as Christ promises they shall be) into the fellowship of him who in the Church is "lifted up" in death and life, in suffering and triumph.

As to just how God's act in raising him from the dead is to be visualized, or even conceived—this is utterly beyond our power. The simple notion that a corpse was revived is inadmissible, not because it is impossible, but because it is irrelevant. It would explain, to be sure, the existence of the living physical body of Jesus after his death (having "flesh and bones," eating with his disciples, and the like). But that is not our problem. What we need is an explanation of how it can be that the one the Church remembers in the flesh it also knows as (or in) the Spirit. And a theory of resuscitation has nothing to do with the case. Even if it could be proved true, we should still have on our hands the unanswered question of how the man Jesus (now brought back from the dead) became the Lord and Christ we know. Shall we say, then, that a dead physical body was gradually or suddenly transformed into a body of some finer substance, which then emerged from the tomb, leaving it empty? The Gospels seem to imply something like this, and one may find such a view implicit in Paul's references to his experience of "seeing" the risen Jesus and in his description of the "spiritual body" God will give those who "die in Christ." If we find such a way of thinking congenial and convincing, well and good; certainly it cannot be refuted. Most modern persons, however, will have difficulty with it.

The fact of the matter is that the question, "How are the dead raised up and with what body do they come?" is a more baffling problem to us than it could have been to the Corinthian Christians. Paul's answer is as good as any we are likely to devise; but if, as we may assume, it did not fully satisfy the Corinthians, certainly it falls even further short of satisfying us. Actually, any picturing of God's act in raising Jesus, any describing of what happened in the sense of what might have been observed to happen when this act took place, is and has always been purely speculative and fanciful. We do not know; we cannot know. Even in the Gospels and Paul, although we may find *implied* some concrete notion of what happened, no one ventures to state it. And in Acts "witnesses of the resurrection" are witnesses to the reality of the risen Christ, not witnesses of his rising. Whatever happened in the way of an observable incident was not a part of the experience of the early Church. No one observed it, no one even claims to have observed it—and actually we have no reason whatever for concluding that there was anything capable of being observed.

Is the Resurrection, then, a historical occurrence? If by the term one means this observable incident, the answer is certainly No. Even if such an incident happened, this negative answer would still need to be given, for, however "observable" it may have been, it was not in fact observed; it would actually have happened only in the silence and loneliness of the tomb and therefore quite beyond the boundaries of history. But if by the Resurrection we mean, not the incident of the rising, but the Church's knowing the risen one, then it belongs to history because the Church does. This definition of the Resurrection *insofar as it can be said to belong to history* as "the Church's knowing the risen one" must not be thought of as a reducing of it to something merely subjective; it is not an idea or a way of thinking, whether about Jesus' death or about anything else. It is a *knowing,* and the concrete object of the knowing is as real as the knowing itself. The same thing is true, of course, of our knowledge of anyone or anything. To say that something exists only in, or that it does not exist beyond, our knowledge of it would be to say that it does not really exist at all and that therefore our "knowledge" is not knowledge at all. Those who do not share in the Church's knowing may, of course, deny the objectivity of the thing known and the propriety of our using the word "know." My point is that the Church could not conceivably do so. For the Church to doubt this knowledge—that is, to doubt the objectivity of the Resurrection—would be to doubt its own existence.

Nor does the proposed definition mean that the objective

personal reality of him whom we know as Jesus Christ our Lord is thought of, or could be thought of, as confined to the historical Church. We find ourselves speaking of him, and sometimes even addressing him, as sitting "at the right hand of the throne of God," and we expect to see him there. But we actually know him now, not there, but here; not outside history, but within it. The Resurrection, insofar as it can be thought of as historical fact, belongs to the existence of the Church.

The Church came into conscious being when Jesus, alive and exalted after his suffering and death, was made known to those who remembered him. We sometimes speak of the Event as culminating in the Resurrection; but we are just as likely to speak of it as culminating in the coming of the Spirit or in the full self-conscious emergence of the Church. This is not to speak of three things, but of one. Easter and Whitsunday do not celebrate two moments, but one only—the moment when those who remembered Jesus became the community in which he was known as present and living Spirit. To belong to this community is to "know him and the power of his resurrection"; to "know him and the power of his resurrection" is to belong to this community. This is not to identify the Event with the Church—to do so would be to deny the reality of the Event in any distinctive sense—but rather with the *coming into being* of the Church.[2] As such, the Event is both distinguishable from the Church as a continuing historical community and related essentially, integrally, inseparably with it. The first experience of the risen Christ and of the Spirit—one experience, however differently it is being *thought of* when the two phrases are used—marks the climax, the culmination, of that process of the Church's "becoming," which is the Event of Christ.

To say that the Resurrection of Christ, insofar as it belongs to history, took place only within the larger Event of the

[2] On this distinction, see the opening pages of Ch. VI, below.

Church's "becoming" is not to deny its miraculous character —that is, its character as an act of God, a happening beyond any naturalistic or humanistic explanation—provided we recognize the miraculous character of the Church itself. In every part of our discussion thus far this character has been presupposed, and the whole position I am stating would collapse utterly if that basic assumption were removed. I have spoken of the Church as being essentially a community of memory and the Spirit. But the Spirit is not a human spirit, a "natural" or indigenous *esprit de corps;* it is the Spirit of God apprehended also as the very being of the remembered Jesus. When I describe the Church so, I am not seeking to state a theoretical norm; I believe I am doing absolutely nothing beyond describing what we actually know as members of it. This *is* the existential reality of the Church. But how can this be? How can the remembered one be thus known? And how can the one known be thus remembered? How can we explain the fusion of shared memory and shared knowledge which constitutes for us the meaning of "Christ"? How can we explain the inner corporate existence of the Church and the healing and life we find there? Psychology and sociology can give no satisfactory answer—that is, no answer satisfactory to those who know the reality and are therefore alone in position to ask the questions.

Nor is the more objective, and abstract, philosophical question susceptible of any "reasonable" answer. How *can* the Spirit be in fact both the actual presence of God and the actual being of the remembered Jesus? We can think of "the Spirit" as representing God's immanence in distinction from his ultimate "otherness" and transcendence ("the Father"). But not only is there nothing in the idea of God which requires a co-ordinate reference to the human Jesus; logical thought about God can hardly accommodate such a reference. It is not easy to justify on general theoretical grounds a necessary "threeness" in the nature of God; but even if this "threeness" should be established, the problem of identifying the third element in God's essential being with a historical individual would remain, and would remain just as difficult and recalcitrant as before. Actually, however, the "threeness" with which we are really concerned is not in the nature of God as an object of thought, but in the Church's experience of the divine; and here the ground for the trinitarian confession is firmly and amply laid: the Spirit the Church knows is both the transcendent God and the personal reality of Jesus. This being the experiential fact, it was inevitable that the Church should try to work out the logical implications. Its experience seemed inescapably to imply the identity of the risen Jesus with God. But it was hardly conceivable that he should have *become* God. If he were now God, he must always have been God. And so the Church was led by seemingly logical steps to the affirmations about the eternal "Son" or "Logos" which the later doctrine of the Trinity was to embody. But though the steps may have been logical, the conclusion to which they eventually led is no more comprehensible in terms of pure thought than the experiential facts from which the rationalizing process began. The mystery of the Trinity answers to the actual realized identity between three distinguishable realities in the Church's experience: the remembered Master, the living Lord, and God's own presence and power. This realized identity is the miracle of the Resurrection and the Church's creation.

One who belongs to that new creation will find oneself responding to what is disclosed there in some such way as: " 'Blessed be the God and Father of our Lord Jesus Christ,' who has 'called us out of darkness into his marvelous light'! The Church is the corporate reality of Christ, the body of Jesus' Resurrection, the locus of God's presence and saving action! The Church is God's deed, wonderful beyond our understanding! 'Thanks be to God for his unspeakable gift!' " One who speaks so about the Church regards it as a "miracle" in the only true sense of that term. This is what a "miracle" is —a reality to which (however "natural" it may seem to others) one finds oneself responding in some such way. Unless it is understood that I am thinking of the Church as being such a reality, no Christian could possibly find acceptable my definition of the Event as the event of its "becoming."

Needless to say, many who do not find this definition acceptable, who find it woefully inadequate and strangely not to the point, would fully agree with what I have just said about the miraculous character of the Church. They, too, would say, "The Church is God's new creation in Christ." What (it seems to me) they fail to recognize, or to recognize clearly enough, is that when we say this, we say all we need to say as Christians, and indeed all we can say with any assurance. Anything more we say is by way of explicating that one statement. This being true, when we see the miraculous character of the Church and its creation, we see the miraculous character of the whole Event of Christ and do not need to postulate the miraculous in an independent or detached sense at any point within it. Because the whole is a miracle, no part needs to be. Because we know the great miracle, we do not need the smaller ones. Indeed, the great miracle scarcely leaves room for them.

It is not surprising that in an earlier age, less scientific and less critical than our own, this logic did not apply; the realization of the miraculous character of the whole Event worked itself out in a different way. Far from discouraging or precluding the proliferation of miracles, it tended to turn every incident and circumstance within the Event into a separate wonder. That the miracle stories of the Gospels are, by and large, the products of this tendency is unmistakably clear. From Paul's letters, our earliest sources, one would conclude that in the beginning the Church affirmed only the miracle in its own existence—the miracle of the actual realized presence as Lord and Christ of him whom it remembered. The miracle, the only miracle, was "Christ crucified"—the identity of the risen, exalted "Christ" with the remembered one on his Cross. The only "glory" of the human life was the love willing and able to bear the burden of our sins and griefs.

But almost at once the tendency to "supernaturalize" would have begun to have its effect: "Can an event now known to have been so miraculous have failed to disclose its miraculous character at every point?" And with the death of eyewitnesses and the spreading of the preaching outside the original Jewish environment, this tendency would have become less restrained and more productive. The canonical Gospels show us the results of its operation at various stages; and some of the apocryphal Gospels and Acts reveal its final "success"— the career of Jesus emptied of every natural or authentically human fact. Such extreme manifestations of this trend the ancient Church rejected quite as decisively as we find ourselves doing. But there can be no doubt that some of the "wonders" which were not rejected, but became a permanent part of its tradition, were earlier fruits of this same tendency. It is not my intention to discriminate among the miracle stories of the Gospels as between those which represent merely the operation of this creative trend and those which can be regarded as having a solid basis in fact (as, I do not doubt, the stories of healings do), much less to try to state what this "basis in fact" in every case might be. My point is, rather, that the value of all of them lies entirely in the witness they bear to a prior fact, which they have had no part whatever in establishing—namely, the realized presence in the Church of the remembered Jesus. We do not know this fact because we "believe" the miracle stories (that is, accept their literal factual truth); rather, we "believe" the miracle stories (if we do "believe" them) and find them significant (whether we "believe" them or not) because we first know the fact.

I have just said that we may find them significant whether we "believe" them (that is, as factually accurate) or not. One can say more than that: they will be for the Christian *equally* significant in either case. The statement of the Creed, for example, that Jesus was born of the Virgin Mary has exactly the same value for the Christian who doubts that it actually happened thus as for the Christian who accepts the literal truth of the statement with no question whatever, although the latter will probably have some difficulty in recognizing this. He is likely to suppose that his knowledge of the miracle of God's act in Christ is the result, at least in part, of his "belief" in the actual fact of Jesus' supernatural birth, and that therefore his brother, who does not share this "belief," cannot share his knowledge of the greater miracle. But he is mistaken on both counts. Actually, he finds *the literal truth* of the miracle story even acceptable for the same reason his brother finds it dispensable: he has prior knowledge of a miracle which far transcends in scope and depth of significance the Virgin Birth or any similar wonder. For him as well as for his brother the real value of the story lies in its dramatization of the supernatural character of the whole Event.

Such a miracle story may be of the greatest symbolic importance, an actual carrier of the ineffable concrete meaning of the Event. For this reason it may be treasured equally by those who are sure it "happened" and by those who doubt that it did. Both may resist equally strongly the suggestion that it be abandoned or surrendered; but their resistance in both cases—although this may not always be recognized—will stem from concern, not for what the story says, but for what it stands for. Both will suspect, probably rightly, that the proposal to surrender it reflects not simply doubt of the truth of the particular story, but the assumption that the whole Event of Christ and the whole life of the Church can be described and explained in naturalistic or humanistic terms, can be fitted smoothly into the continuities of nature and of history as a part of nature. The Virgin Birth or the empty tomb may be the "flag" around which the battle seems to be raging, but the miraculous character of the Church's existence is the real, the only substantial issue.

The Resurrection of Jesus, however, is more than a symbol of this miracle of the Church's life—more than the Virgin

Birth and the empty tomb, which, whether they are thought of as "happening" or not, must be recognized as having only symbolic significance. The Resurrection of Jesus is a fact of the objective order, both indubitable and essential. This cannot be said of any of the miracle stories—including the miracle stories which confirm or illustrate the Resurrection itself. The story of Jesus' Virgin Birth, whether factually true or not, once having been introduced into the tradition, soon achieved a place there from which it would be difficult, if not impossible, to dislodge it. But it is conceivable, easily conceivable, that the story might never have been told at all. In that event, the Church would now lack one of its historic symbols, but would otherwise not be poorer. Perhaps some other story about Jesus' birth would have taken its place in the tradition and would have come to have precisely the same symbolic value. The same kind of thing can be said of the story of the empty tomb and of some of the encounters of the risen Jesus with his disciples, for example, the walk and conversation he had with two of his disciples going to Emmaus. It is conceivable that these stories might never have been told, whether because the incidents narrated did not actually happen or for some other reason. Perhaps other stories, testifying equally impressively to the Resurrection, would have survived in their stead. In that event, not only would the Church not know that it lacked anything; it would not in fact lack anything. All such stories have value, not as evidence of anything we should not otherwise know, but as eloquent reminders and signs of something we know already.

But the Resurrection of Jesus is not of this kind. It is not a story which the Christian may find credible or incredible. It is not subject to confirmation or invalidation by historical research. It does not merely illustrate or exemplify the miraculous nature of the event, in the way all miracle stories do, so that some other story might conceivably do as well. Actually, we have to do here, not with a story at all, although stories, sagas and legends soon grew up about it, but with an essential implication of the existence of the Church itself. I do not mean merely that one cannot explain or account for the Church without positing the Resurrection; I mean that one cannot belong to the Church without knowing the concrete meaning, what Paul calls the "power," of the Resurrection. Both the human life of Jesus and his Resurrection must be thought of as objective facts, however unimaginable the latter may be —facts belonging to the Church's past. But just as we have contact with Jesus through the Church's memory, so in the continuing experience of the Spirit we are actually confronted by the living, and therefore the "raised," Christ. The Church affirms the Resurrection because its own existence as the community of memory and the Spirit is the essential and continuing meaning of the Resurrection.

Paul Tillich has written: "Christianity was born, not with the birth of the man who is called 'Jesus,' but in the moment in which one of his followers was driven to say to him, 'Thou art the Christ.' "[3] The reference—taken symbolically, of course—is to the incident narrated in Mark as occurring at Caesarea Philippi just before Jesus' final journey to Jerusalem. Agreeing as I profoundly do with Tillich's emphasis upon the response of faith as belonging essentially to the objective Event of Christ, I should yet say that a better moment to symbolize the birth of Christianity can be found in the Gospels. It is the moment when *after Jesus' death* a group of his disciples recognize in a divine Presence, wonderfully new and strange, the very one they have known and loved: "It is the Lord" (John 21:7). In this moment of recognition the Resurrection (whatever it may be conceived to have been in and of itself) became for the first time a historical fact, and the Church, which had been in process of "becoming" since Jesus' first disciples were gathered about him, came finally into actual being.

[3] *Systematic Theology*, II, p. 97.

IV *The Church and the Incarnation*

MANY TIMES IN THE COURSE OF THIS DISCUSSION I HAVE referred to the Event as the locus or medium of a creative "deed" of God. God "acted" in Christ. Sometimes, theologians speak of him as "breaking into history"—a phrase, not too fortunate, but suggesting both the historical character of the mode of the action and the transcendent, divine nature of the action itself. This conviction that the God of all nature and history and of the heavens beyond, in an action without parallel, entered into man's life with mighty power in a particular historical happening is one of the most intimate convictions of the Church.

The grounds for this conviction lie entirely within the Church itself. Since the Event, as we have seen, is by definition the coming into being of the Church, any convictions we may have about its value or significance are basically convictions about the Church and, if sound, rest on realities within its existence. If the Event can be called a "saving" event, it is only because the Church is found to be a "saving" community. If God can be said to have "acted" in the Event, it is only because the Church makes itself known to us as a divine creation. I mean, not merely that we should not *know about* the Event and God's action in it if it were not for the Church, but that without the Church the Event would not have occurred and the action would not have taken place. I mean, not merely that nothing distinctively Christian could be *known* except in and through the Church, but that nothing distinctively Christian would exist in such a case.

Although this statement has been made in effect many times and indeed is implicit in this whole discussion, it may still seem excessively strong; and perhaps we should again pay some attention to objections which may be made to it. Someone says: "What about God's reality? Surely that is important to the Christian. And who would claim that it can be known only within the Church, much less that God exists only there?" Put in this way, the question is capable only of the expected answer. But suppose we are asking the question, as I believe we usually are, not about God in some very general sense, but about "the God and Father of our Lord Jesus Christ"? Must we not recognize that this reality is known only within the Church? How, indeed, could it be known anywhere else? It is by definition a historically revealed reality—a reality that became known in a historical event or in the course of a historical development which culminated in that event. This is not to say, I repeat, that God can be known only as revealed in this history, or even that he can be best known there (although the Christian can hardly help believing this), but simply that he is differently or distinctively known there. He is known there as he is known nowhere else, and when we refer to "the God and Father of our Lord Jesus Christ" we are referring to God as thus known.

"But," the objector may continue, "granted the particularity and concreteness of this revelation of God, that it occurred in and through a unique Event, surely you cannot mean to affirm that this Event can be known, much less that it occurred, only within the Church." Yet this is precisely what can be, and must be, affirmed. To be sure, something happened in Palestine in the middle part of the first century which was a matter of general notice and perhaps of public record. The historical career of Jesus ending with his Crucifixion under Pontius Pilate is a fact beyond any possible denial. But although this career occurred—and it is important to recognize that it did—it can hardly be called a historical event, if by that term we mean an incident with important historical consequences. The career of Jesus is certainly not such an event in Jewish history or in Roman; it is such an event only in Hebrew-Christian history. Even those who question this statement will not deny that only in that history—indeed, only in *Christian* history—is it the particular Event it is. The career of Jesus as it might be conceived of apart from the particular responses actually made to him by his disciples, apart from the concrete meanings found in it by what proved to be the incipient Church—the career, thus separated from this context, would be an abstraction, not an event at all, certainly not the Event to which the Church traces its own beginning. That Event is knowable solely within the Church; furthermore, by definition it can have occurred only within its life.

It may seem at first that to speak so is to place the actuality of the Event in jeopardy. In truth, however, it is the only possible way of securing it. If the Event is thought of as simply antedating the Church, as participating not at all in the Church's own existence, as something purely "objective" or "factual," occurring before the Church began and merely providing the occasion of its beginning—in such a case, we are in the position either of being dependent upon historical science—archaeological findings and the like—for any knowledge we can have of it, or else of accepting some particular account of it "by faith." We have already seen that we are simply not in the first of these positions—the position of looking wistfully to the excavations of the archaeologists, or the explorations of the paleographers, or the studies of the historians to see whether we can continue to be Christians or not! But our position would be equally insecure in the second case. For the "faith" which gives us answers to historical questions is not faith at all. Faith is our response to God's reality confronting us in our actual existence; it is not a

credulous or superstitious acceptance of happenings reputed
to have occurred in the past. By whatever name assurance of
the latter kind is called, we have no right to it, and in the
long run it must fail us. The situation actually is that the
Church both knows beyond peradventure that the Event
occurred and knows equally surely what its significance was;
and it can know all of this because the Event actually took
place within its emerging life.

The intimate and integral involvement within the very
existence of an event of the meanings found in it by those
among whom or to whom it occurs is familiar in our common
life and could be endlessly illustrated. How often it happens
that an incident, trivial and negligible in common regard,
is for some one person a profoundly significant crisis! Something happened publicly, yes—the whole neighborhood knew
about it—but *the event* happened only to him! Or perhaps it is
an experience within a family. The death of a child, let us
say, has the effect of creating an entirely new spirit in a family,
of binding its members together in a new unity, of revealing
to them a new depth of meaning in the whole of life. The
child's death is in one sense a public occurrence—a record is
made of it on the city's register, and notice of various kinds
is taken of it by neighbors and friends. But nowhere else is
the death the revealing, transforming, perhaps even redeeming, event it is for the family itself.

It would be quite impossible in such a case for an analyst,
inside the family or outside, to identify clearly or exhaustively
the reasons why this incident should have been for these persons just the event it was. Almost certainly he would cite the
character of the child as he was intimately known within the
family circle, various poignant memories of him shared by
the group, the love which had been felt for him, the hopes
that had been wrapped up in him. Equally surely reference
would be made to various elements in the general family situation, particularly at the time when the child's death occurred.
But the analysis would never be fully successful. Certainly

those to whom the event occurred would not find it so. And one must finally be content with saying that at a crucial moment in the life of this family—"in the fullness of time"— an incident occurred which, for reasons we cannot fully discern or understand, had meanings and effects for the members of the family so unique in degree and kind that an event can be said to have happened there which occurred nowhere else.

In the same way, the Event of which the Christian speaks occurred only in the Church, and any concrete meanings and values we ascribe to it are ascribed, not merely because we happen to find them there, but because they do not exist, and have never existed, anywhere else. The whole meaning of Christ *as historical Event* is embodied in the Church.

To say this is to say that the Church is "the body of Christ." And, indeed, I believe the basic meaning of these words as applied to the Church lies in the fact of its thus "embodying" the Event. The phrase is found first in Paul, and in what may appear at first glance to be a mere metaphor. He is writing to the Corinthian church, which is divided by many factions and is sick with jealousy and strife. To enforce his plea that such a state of things is both inappropriate and destructive, Paul uses the example or analogy of the human body. Here, too, there are "many members"; but they belong to "one body" and have significance only because they do. Each member has its own distinctive "gift" or function, and the body would not be the body if even one of them were missing. The eye is no more surely vital and indispensable than the ear, the hand than the foot. If one organ suffers, all the organs suffer; if one flourishes, the whole body rejoices. It is unthinkable that the eye should say to the hand, "I do not need you"; or the head to the feet, "I do not need you." The appropriateness of this analogy for Paul's practical purpose is obvious enough, and he very skillfully applies it in this passage (I Cor. 12:12-31). It is clear, however, that it occurs to him at all only because he thinks of the Church as being "the body of Christ" in a more realistic sense. "We were all baptized into one body," he writes near the beginning of the passage; and at its end, "You are the body of Christ." More is involved here than a mere comparison. The Church is not merely *like* a body; it is *in fact* the body of Christ. This sense of the phrase appears unmistakably in the Epistles to the Colossians and the Ephesians, which, whether written by Paul or another, set forth in this respect the authentically Pauline view. But however this may be, the phrase undoubtedly states what has been the Church's most characteristic and persistent view of itself from the first century until now.

No image could be more apt or adequate. "The body of Christ" suggests the definitive, tangible, "visible" nature of the Church—a particular, concrete, historical reality. It expresses the character of the Church as organic community, a living social whole, which could not exist without its parts but cannot be simply identified with the sum of them. It conveys the quality of the Christian existence as a sharing, a participation, in an objective corporate existence. It suggests something of the vocation of the Church—to serve as Christ's agent or instrument. It corresponds closely with the Christian's characteristic way of realizing his relation with Christ: he belongs to Christ, not in the relatively simple way in which one person may be bound in loyalty to another, but in the sense of being immersed, as it were, in another's being. He can describe this relation most fully by saying, not "for Christ," or "with Christ," but "in Christ." When he does so, he is saying in effect that the Church is Christ's "body": membership in the Church is membership "in Christ."

This brings us very close to the meaning of the phrase which is both most fundamental or central and most pertinent to this particular discussion: By "body" we ordinarily mean the spatial-temporal locus of personal existence and the medium of its expression; and when we speak of the Church as "the body of Christ," we are using the term in just that sense. Christ is present in the Church in the same way a man is present in his body. Without a body one could not belong to this realm of space and time, of nature and history; neither could Christ. To speak, therefore, of the Church as the body of Christ is to say something definitive, not only about the Church, but also about Christ. The Church is not one of his bodies or a part of his body. It *is* his body, if by "body" we mean something human and historical, something made of man's substance, his flesh and heart. The Church is the historical locus, the "embodiment," of God's saving action within the temporal order. The corporate reality of the Christian Church is in the most literal and realistic sense possible the body of Christ.

Thus far we have not used the word "incarnation," but it is obvious that the *idea* of incarnation has been fully present in all that has been said. To say that God's saving act was and is embodied in the Church's existence is to say (if we wish to use the term in that connection) that it is "incarnate" there. Actually, however, we have not ordinarily wished to apply the word in that way. We have reserved it to designate the human life of Jesus our Lord: he himself in the days of his flesh was "God incarnate." How, then, do we see the relation of this "incarnation" to the "embodiment" which we affirm to have taken place in the Church? Have we to do with two "bodies"—the body of his flesh, his own discrete existence as a man, and his body, the Church? Was God in Christ twice incarnated—first in Jesus and then in the Church? Or are we to think somehow of Jesus' human existence as being *God's* "body," and the Church as being the "body" of the risen *Christ*? None of these possibilities is likely to appeal to us, whether stated thus crudely or described in more sophisticated ways. We know that there is no reason to affirm more than one Incarnation; indeed, that there is every reason for affirming one only. The way of preserving the unity here to which we most frequently resort is to call the Church "the extension of the Incarnation." The difficulty with this phrase is not that it says too much for the Church, but too little; it suggests that the Incarnation antedated the Church or took place outside it; and therefore it does not do full justice to the "embodiment," the "incarnation," which was, and is, the Church itself.

I should like to suggest two steps toward the solution of this problem. The first lies in the recognition that in the tradition of the Church, the Incarnation has most frequently been referred to as the Incarnation of the Word. Without becoming involved in the intricacies of trinitarian controversy, we may say that when we use the phrase "the Word of God," we are speaking of the creative, revealing, redeeming *action* of God. The meaning of this truth in the present connection appears most clearly and consistently in the work of W. Norman Pittenger, to whom I am greatly indebted. In *The Word Incarnate* he writes: "The Word or Logos [is the] Self-Expressive Activity of God"; and the christology of that important book is the working out of the implications of that sentence.[1] The Incarnation, then, is not to be thought of as a static thing, the divine substance becoming visible and tangible (a way of thinking which leads almost inevitably, and whether we recognize it or not, to some kind of Docetism), but, dynamically, as the bodying forth of God's *action* in history. This action had its center in the personal existence of Jesus of Nazareth. It took place in him and through him. It is this fact that makes him absolutely unique among men. To quote Norman Pittenger again: "Jesus, then, is truly human; he is truly divine. The divine in him is God at work in and through him, the act of God which he is. . . ."[2] He *is* "the Word Incarnate"—not in the sense of being the solidification, as it were, or "congealing," of some ethereal substance, but rather in the sense of being the dynamic personal medium of God's saving action.

[1] New York: Harper & Brothers, 1959, p. 187.
[2] *Christ and Christian Faith* (New York: Round Table Press, 1941), p. 66. I have quoted these words in another book, but they more than deserve the repetition.

God acted "for us men and our salvation" through an authentic human life. The embodiment of that action in that life is what we mean by "the Incarnation."

The second step, which follows closely upon the first, is the recognition that the human career of Jesus did not antedate the Church, but lay entirely within the period and the process of its beginning. The historical Event which had its decisive center in Jesus was in its totality the coming into being of the Church. One will not say that God acted in Jesus and *then* created the Church. To speak of his action in and through Jesus and of his action in creating the Church is to speak of the same action. His action in and through Jesus *was* his creation of the Church. If, then, we are to think of the Incarnation as the embodying or "enfleshing" of the *action* of God in history, we have to do here, not with two "incarnations," or even with one "extended," but with one only. The "embodying" of God's action in Jesus and the "embodying" of his action in bringing the Church into being is one embodying of one action.

In the second chapter of this book I indicated something of the way Jesus himself is remembered in the Church. He is recognized as having been good and great beyond what we should otherwise have dreamed possible for man. No one who senses his greatness would try to describe it; and only in the terms of poetry and art can its quality even be suggested. Men called him "Master" and "Lord," and they did well, for such he was. This recognition of the incomparable moral and spiritual grandeur of the man Christ Jesus has belonged to the Church from the beginning and is an inalienable element in its memory of him. Moreover, this recognition belongs inseparably with our recognition of God's saving deed in him. The supreme goodness of Jesus was an essential—perhaps, if comparisons in such a matter are possible at all, the most centrally essential—factor in the Event. Nor can we think of it as merely fortuitous, as though God "happened" to find a good man of whom to make use in accomplishing his purpose in history. On the contrary, the goodness of Jesus can itself be explained only as belonging to God's creating, saving deed. And yet would we not all agree that this deed did not take place in his individual being in some detached, static, or purely intrinsic sense? It took place in him in the midst of his own, and involved action, reaction, and interaction, as all human existence does. It took place in the concrete body of relationships in which he stood to certain ones about him, and they to him and to one another in his presence. It took place in the creation through and around him of a new and very particular kind of human community. In a word, it took place in the coming into being of the Church. The corporate reality of the Church is the "body" of God's action in Christ.

We reach the same conclusion if we proceed by a slightly different route: Most of us would agree, I believe, that "the Incarnation" is a way of referring to the Event as the medium of the redemptive act of God in Christ. But this Event, as we have so often seen, was, like all events and indeed like all concrete things, immeasurably rich and complex. It did not occur, simply and fully, in the moment of Jesus' birth; surely, it included his own maturing as a human being and his life with others and with God. And who would think of denying that it included also his death and his Resurrection? But to speak of his Resurrection is already to have spoken of the new community, in whose life the memory of Jesus was miraculously fused with the awareness of his living reality and presence. The Event cannot be said to have taken place until this miracle had occurred—that is, until the Resurrection. But if the Incarnation is another way of referring to this same Event, it too cannot have occurred earlier—although it will have been in process of occurring all the while. "Incarnation," to be sure, *says* something about the Event which other terms do not say: God came to us in Christ "in great humility"; "the Word became flesh"; "he was made man." These statements are for the Christian both true and supremely significant.

But insofar as they are statements about history, they refer to realities within the existence of the Church, in whose creation God's action in Christ was bodied forth.

If we see the Church as being in very fact the body of Christ, we shall see the various stages in the development of its christology as steps in the progressive realization and explication of this fact. This process of discovery and understanding involved what can only be called the gradual "mythologizing" of the Event. Because of the usual connotation of the term "myth," the Christian is often not prepared to see and acknowledge its appropriateness as applied to precious items in his confession of faith. Actually, however, much in his confession has this character and, moreover, could not in the nature of the case have any other. For "myth" is our only way, not only of expressing and conveying to others, but also of realizing for ourselves, the divine meaning of an experience. The growing myth, the developing saga or story, may represent, and often does represent, a deepening realization of this meaning; and therefore the more advanced the mythology, the more true—that is, the more adequately representative— it may be. The developing story will inevitably find us moving further and further from the *time* of the original experience and perhaps from the bare facts of it, but it may be bringing us nearer and nearer to its meaning. The simplest, most general, way of affirming the divine character of an experience is to say, "God was present" or "God acted." But even this statement, simple as it is, cannot be regarded as a plain statement of fact, since God transcends both space and time and therefore cannot be said to "be present" or to "act" in any literal sense of those terms. If we speak so—as we must if we speak at all—our statement, whether we recognize it or not, partakes of the character of a "story." If we would express the divine meaning of the experience more fully or precisely, or even realize it more fully or precisely ourselves, our "story" must become more elaborate and detailed; but it is now no more and no less a "story" than it has been all along. We may speak of God as a mere object of thought, a mere term in a philosophical construction, without resort to this kind of discourse (although even this is more difficult than we often suppose); but any statement about God's relations with us, about his "presence" or "action" in nature or history, must needs be mythological in character.[3] It is not by chance, then, that the Church's attempts to realize and convey the divine meaning of its own existence took the form of a story; there was no other form it could conceivably take.

It was almost as inevitable that the story should have been a story about Jesus and that the Church's distinctive theology should have been a christology. Jesus had been the decisive center of the action of the Event. What had happened had happened entirely in and around him. The Church's memory of its beginnings was a memory of him. Moreover, the same Jesus, living and present, was the personal center of the Church's continuing existence. It would have been, is, and must always be impossible to speak of either the Event or the Church without speaking of him. The story of God's action was, and had to be, *his* story. If the Event had (in the actual existence of the Church) proved to be the "saving" Event, it could only be because he was, in his own individual person, the Savior. If the Event could be adequately described as nothing less than

[3] W. Norman Pittenger (*The Word Incarnate*, pp. 33-44) raises a question about the propriety of using the word "myth" as "an omnibus word to describe this sort of religious language." He believes that it should be restricted to representations of realities beyond history or of a general or universal kind—such as the "fall" of man or the eschatological consummation—and that the term "story" or "saga" should be used of the Incarnation and the Atonement, both of which were accomplished *"in* history and through the factuality of *particular* historical happenings." I am convinced that this suggestion is sound, but know that I have not been consistent in following it. I find it much more natural to say "story" in speaking of God's action in Christ. There is, however, no obvious synonym for "mythology" or "mythological"; therefore this word, both noun and adjective, comes to have almost necessarily an inclusive or "omnibus" character. This being true, it is hard to avoid using "myth," at least sometimes, in the broader and less precise way.

a "divine" Event (a locus of God's "acting" or "working"), it could only be because Jesus was, in his own nature, a divine person. In a word, all the realized values in the new corporate existence tended to locate themselves in *his* existence; the whole meaning of both Event and Church was expressed, and, it was felt, could only be expressed, in affirmations about *him,* his "nature" and "work." In such a situation, not only was the door open to the increasing mythologization of Jesus' human career, but the impulsion to move in that direction was quite irresistible.

It is noteworthy, however, that the first titles given to Jesus correspond very closely with the first realized meanings of the Event within the primitive community. He was called "Lord" and "Christ." Each of these terms designates, primarily and basically, not an intrinsic character of Jesus—the terms are not of that kind—but a relationship in which he was seen to stand to Event and Church. He was called "Lord" because he was in fact "the Lord," the Church's "Lord"; he was remembered as such by his disciples, and as such, in a transfigured sense, he was now known. Whatever other meanings the title soon acquired, it began in the Church's awareness of the relation in which it stood to him; he was known as "our Lord" before he was thought of as being, or as destined to be, "Lord" in some more general, or in the absolute, sense.[4] Similarly, the title "Christ" represented in the first instance the Church's recognition of the relation of Jesus to the Event. In this Event, God had "visited and redeemed his people." What the first Christians had witnessed was nothing less than

---

[4] I recognize that this way of understanding the earliest use of the word "Lord" cannot be demonstrated, but it is, a priori, most likely, and is at least strongly indicated by the *maran atha* of I Cor. 16:22. I have defended the proposed understanding in *The Early Church and the Coming Great Church* (Nashville: Abingdon Press, 1955), pp. 71 ff., and have cited there other literature. Not cited is an article on "Lord" by J. Y. Campbell in A. Richardson, *A Theological Word Book of the Bible* (New York: The Macmillan Company, 1951), where the same understanding is favored. See also E. Schweizer, *Lordship and Discipleship* (London: SCM Press, 1960), p. 58.

the eschatological Event, "the great and manifest day," in which God was fulfilling his promises to Israel, pouring out his "Spirit on all flesh," bestowing "visions" and "prophecy," showing "wonders in the heaven above and signs in the earth beneath." This was the "manifest" character of the Event. Could Jesus, then, who had so completely dominated it, in and around whom alone it had occurred, be other than "the Christ"? The Church did not come into being because of a prior belief that Jesus was "Lord and Christ." Rather, this belief itself came into being because it answered to the realities of the Church's existence. It was a community in which Jesus was actually known as "Lord" and whose own character as the locus of God's redeeming action required that he be recognized as "Christ."

Further evidence of this correlation between the Church's christology and its self-awareness lies in the fact that in the earliest form of the "story," these titles were first bestowed on Jesus at his Resurrection. It was *then* that he was "made Lord and Christ." But this was also the time when the community first came into self-conscious existence. Its first awareness of "the Lord Jesus Christ" was also its first awareness of itself; its awareness of itself was nothing other than its awareness of him. One may object: "Yes, this is true of its *awareness*; but, *in actual fact,* Jesus, and even his Resurrection, must be thought of as both prior to the community and independent of it." This can be granted about Jesus in some general objective sense, with which historical science may concern itself, and even about the Resurrection in some objective sense quite beyond our knowing (and it should be noted that in what I am going to say these "objective" facts and their importance are being taken for granted), but it is decidedly *not* true of "our Lord Jesus Christ." The particular concrete reality denoted by that phrase exists only for the Church and within it. Each of these terms, not to speak of the even more distinctive relationship among them, answers to something within the existence of the Church and has its characteristic meaning

in no other connection. "Jesus" is Jesus as the Church remembers him; "Lord" designates the same one known as
present living Spirit; and "Christ," God's saving action in
bringing the new community into being through him and
around him.

It is not enough, nor is it true, to say that although we
know these realities only within the Church, they exist, "of
course," also outside—any more than it would be true to
say that "mother" in my family exists outside although we
know her only there. Our mother is "mother"—that is, the particular person whom this word names for us—only among us,
her children. This obviously does not mean that simply as a
human being she has no existence apart from us; or that she
may not be well known, even intimately known, by others;
or that the ground of her relationship with us is not firmly laid
in certain biological and sociological facts of a quite "objective" character. But though she is, and is known to be, our
mother in this purely factual sense, yet she is "mother" only
because we respond to her in a particular way and she to us.
She has no reality as "mother" prior to, or independent of,
our reality as her "sons" and "daughters." My awareness of
her as my "mother" and my awareness of myself as her "son"
is really one awareness, and the fact of her being "mother"
and of my being "son" is really one fact.

In the same way, and with the same obvious stipulations as
to the "objective" elements involved, one must recognize that
"our Lord Jesus Christ" has no existence outside the Church
(on earth or in heaven). It was, therefore, a sound instinct
which led the primitive community to describe the moment
of its birth as the moment when God made the Jesus it
remembered "both Lord and Christ." The story of his "adop-
tion" was the inner truth of its own existence. Those who were
"no people" had been made "God's people." Lost in "darkness," they had been "called into his marvelous light." Estranged and divided, they had been given "power to become
the sons of God." This is what had happened in their own
history when God raised Jesus from the dead, saying to him,

"Thou art my Son; this day I have begotten thee," and seating him at his own right hand "in the heavenly places."

But although this primitive "adoptionism" corresponded more closely perhaps than any later christology with the actual experience of the earliest Church, which remembered Jesus as a man and now knew him as Lord and Christ, it did not prove to be the final form of the story. The concrete meaning of Jesus' Lordship within the Church's life, the adoration it found itself offering him, seemed hardly compatible with the "adoptionist" view of his origin as a "simple" man. Besides, reflection, moving backward from the Resurrection, tended to invest his death and then his whole career with a super-natural character. Even earlier, perhaps, pre-existence was affirmed of him. He was identified first with the pre-existing heavenly Son of Man of the apocalyptists and later with the always existing heavenly Wisdom or Logos of the sages. His action in becoming man was thought of first as an act of *kenosis*, a divine being surrendering his divine powers; and later as an act of incarnation, the Logos being actually embodied in Jesus' flesh. This is not the place for any attempt at tracing this development in christology. That it began with "adoptionism" and ended with "incarnationism" is hardly open to doubt; how we should trace the progress be-tween is less clear. But all such questions can be left to the side. My only present point is that the whole development of thought about Jesus' "nature" and "work," insofar as it is concerned with anything belonging to history and the life of man and therefore with anything we can know about or even care about—this whole development has to do with the nature of the Church and with what God offers us there.

We may assess the christological "story," during the whole course of its growth from the first stage to the last, in one of two possible ways: either the Church was indulging in mere fantasy, its whole story of Jesus as the Christ being the product of the sheerest fancy and entirely without claim to truth of any kind, or else the Church was seeking to express with some adequacy the wonder of what God had done, was doing, and was promising to do, in its own existence. The Christian "story" answers to realities disclosed in the Church's life, or it answers to nothing at all. It has its ground in the Church's existence, or it is utterly groundless. Actually it does answer to the Church's experience and is grounded in its life. The Incarnation is affirmed because it has occurred. The Word did become flesh and dwell in the midst of men. God's saving action *was* "bodied forth" in a visible, tangible human Event and has continuing existence in the corporate being of the Church. For the Church is the body of the Resurrection, and to belong to it in truth is to share in the very substance of Christ's new life with God.

The recognition that the conception and birth of Jesus as Lord and Christ was also the conception and birth of the Church; that the Incarnation was not a static thing to be identified with the "nature," or with something in the "nature," of the human Jesus, but was the historical "bodying forth" (and is still the embodiment) of God's redemptive action in Christ—this recognition should have at least two liberating effects. It should relieve the Gospel tradition of an impossible pressure, and it should free the humanity of Jesus from an intolerable strain. Each of these points needs to be briefly discussed.

It should be noted first, then, that the locating of the Incarnation, as a kind of static thing, in the individual personal existence of Jesus has brought the Gospel tradition under an arbitrary pressure which that tradition is simply not able to bear. One can see this pressure at work even in the period of the composition of the Gospels. As we move from Mark, through Matthew and Luke, to John, we can see the effort of the community, no less real for being unintentional and unconscious, to bring the account of Jesus' career into agreement with the developing belief that Jesus was God—to make the facts of history fit the view that in him, in his own discrete being, the Eternal Word became an actual human individual. But this effort did not succeed. Even in the Fourth Gospel, where it is carried furthest, some inconsistent "facts" recalcitrantly remain; and Mark is full of them.

But if, in the period of the growing and still unfixed tradition, the Church's developing view of Jesus as being himself the Incarnation (in the sense of a human personalization of God's being) could not obliterate the sure evidences that the original facts did not support such a view, surely we cannot hope at this late date to "interpret" these same evidences away. The Gospels, even as they stand, do not present us with such an individual as the identification of the Incarnation in this sense with Jesus simply and alone would require us to find. Read with any critical intelligence, they fail even more obviously to do so. Nor does the "memory" of the Church help to make up this deficiency. The Church does not "remember" the "Word made flesh"; it "remembers" the human Jesus, great and good and dying on a cross. If it knows the "Word made flesh" (as of course it does!), it knows it in its own existence, where alone, so far as history is concerned, Christ in his fullness (which certainly includes the Resurrection) is embodied.

But more serious than the arbitrary coercive pressure exerted by the more "static" conception of the Incarnation upon the Gospels is the strain under which it places the humanity of Jesus. Jesus is required to be not only what the Gospels do not represent him to have been, but also what as a human being he could not have been. The ancient Church, struggling with the problem of expressing and communicating, and (in the face of various destructive or reductive interpretations) of defining and defending, the meaning of Christ in its own existence—the ancient Church, struggling with this problem, came finally to affirm the union of two complete natures, human and divine, in one personal existence.[5] Such a definition of Christ's "nature" can be defended

[5] It may be worthwhile to repeat the terms of the "Chalcedonian formula": "Following the holy Fathers we all with one consent teach men to confess

as more adequate than any of the many alternative definitions, which, trying to soften the logical contradiction or to bring the dogma more into line with the Gospel picture of Jesus or with historical probabilities generally, succeed only in reducing the wonder, or distorting the character, of what God has done in Christ. This is true of all the ancient christological heresies, which qualified and thus denied one or the other of the two "natures," and is quite as true of those modern interpreters who in various ways explain the Incarnation as meaning the presence in Jesus *in an extraordinary degree,* or *absolutely,* of some authentically and typically human character or capability.

None of these alternative definitions of Christ's "person" is as good as the ancient one the Councils worked out, for the reason that none of them is as adequate to the reality they are all concerned with, namely, the concrete meaning of the Church's existence as known from within. No reducing of the human or of the divine, no compromising of the full reality of either, no lightening of the contradiction between them, no weakening of the containing unity—none of these can be tolerated. For the Church *knows* "the human"—knows it in the humanity of the Jesus it remembers, knows it in the human event in which it was born, knows it in its own being as a human community. It also *knows* "the divine"—knows

---

one and the same Son, our Lord Jesus Christ, the same perfect in deity and perfect in humanity, God truly and man truly, of a reasonable soul and body, of one substance with the Father in his deity, and of one substance with us in his humanity, in all things like unto us without sin; begotten before the ages of the Father in his deity, in the last days for us and for our salvation born of Mary the virgin, the God-bearer, in his humanity; one and the same Christ, Son, Lord, only begotten, acknowledged in two natures, without confusion, without change, without division, without separation; the distinction of the natures being by no means taken away because of the union, but rather the characteristics of each nature being preserved and coming together in one person and one hypostasis, not divided or separated into two persons but one and the same Son and only begotten God Logos, Lord Jesus Christ; as from the beginning the prophets and the Lord Jesus Christ himself taught us concerning him, and the creed of the Fathers handed down to us."

it in the coming of the Spirit, knows it in the miracle of the very presence within it of Christ Crucified, knows it in God's forgiving, reconciling, healing love poured out. Both the "human" and the "divine" are fully, indubitably, present in the Church's experience; moreover, the two are not separated, but they are not the same. So long, then, as the meaning of its life is to be set forth in terms of a definition of Christ's "person," no statement about him will suffice which falls short of affirming both the unity of his personal existence and the full, unqualified reality of two distinct natures in him.

But, for all that, the statement is not fully satisfactory because of the manifest impossibility of a truly human existence actually having this character. I pointed out a moment ago that the "static" conception of the Incarnation requires that Jesus be not only what the Gospels do not represent him to have been, but also what as a human being he could not have been. May I now add that it requires him to be what we would not have wanted him to be—what indeed we cannot bear to think of him as being? For, though we say what we most intimately know when we affirm that *"God* was in Christ," we know that the full, unqualified humanity of Jesus our Lord is equally precious—that we should be denying *him* if we denied it. This the Church in its right mind has always known and has not failed to say from the very beginning. But can we affirm this humanity in the realistic sense in which we must affirm it—can we hold fast our memory of him as "made like his brethren in every respect," sharing, in the whole range of his conscious and subconscious life, our human existence, his joys our joys, our griefs his griefs—can we hold this fast and at the same time think of him as having also another "nature," which was not human at all?

The way to solve this problem is not through attempts to modify the traditional definition of the "nature" of Christ so as to make that definition more credible or even more intelligible. These attempts, as we have seen, only weaken the statement and make it less adequate. The solution lies, rather, in the recognition that the most appropriate form for holding and conveying the meaning of Christ is not a definition of him, but a story about him—the story of the Son of God who "emptied himself" and took the nature of a "servant," who was "obedient unto death, even death on a cross," whom God has "highly exalted" and made "Lord" over Sin and Death. This story was the theology of the earliest Church, its Gospel or "Good News," and no abstract statement could take its place or can ever do so. The concrete meaning of what God did in Christ cannot be expressed in the definition of a hypostasis; it must be "told" as the story of an action. The definition in this case can be true, in the sense of shutting out other definitions less apt and adequate, and can be valuable, even indispensable, in guaranteeing the proper recognition of elements and proportions in the concrete meaning of Christ which might otherwise be obscured; but the fuller truth and the larger value must always remain with the story, where the inner reality of the Event—"things into which angels long to look"—was first expressed and where alone the ineffable fullness of its concrete meaning can be declared.

This does not mean, I repeat, that the Church cannot speak of the "humanity" and the "divinity" of Christ, and, moreover, use both terms without reservation or qualification of any kind, in their true sense and with their full force. Not only is it able to do so, but it would deny itself if it did not. Both terms belong essentially to its message because both elements belong essentially to its life. To deny the humanity would be to deny the Jesus it remembers; to deny the divinity would be to deny the Lord and Christ it knows. To deny the humanity would also be to deny the truly human character of its own existence, and to deny the divinity would be to deny the reality of God's action in creating and sustaining its life. The Church affirms both the humanity and the divinity and, furthermore, affirms them "without confusion" or mingling and without any softening of the distinction between them. It affirms them because it is itself as a human community the "living temple" of the divine Presence, the very Body of Christ, in whom "all the fulness of God is pleased to dwell" with men.

V *The Church and the Atonement*

SINCE THE BEGINNING OF THIS BOOK WE HAVE BEEN considering what has been called the "action" of God in history, the "deed" of God in Christ; and not infrequently some reminder of the value or effect of that "action" has been given. It has been referred to as a "saving," or "redemptive," or "reconciling" act. We must now consider, somewhat more fully and carefully, just what we mean when we say that what happened in the Event, what God did in Christ, was done "for us men and for our salvation."

The participle "reconciling" has been used probably more often than any other to describe this action of God, and there can be no doubt that it comes nearest to doing so with adequacy and truth. No more authentic account of the effect of the Event has been given than Paul's statement: "In Christ God was reconciling the world to himself" (II Cor. 5:18 [mg.]). Not only was this the form which salvation in Christ took; it is the form which salvation *must* take if it is to be salvation at all. For man's desperate need —and mortal peril—lie in his estrangement. This need and peril are writ large in history in the separations and bitter hostilities of nations, races and classes of men, in their exclusive prides, their mutual rejections, their cruel internecine struggles. But these are only the more overt manifestations of Man's plight.

We do not usually think of the author of the Epistle of James as a man of subtle discernments, but he is seeing deeply into truth when he asks: "What causes wars, and what causes fightings among you? Is it not your passions that are at war in your members?" (4:1). Probably we would not want to find a simple "cause and effect" relation here. But we recognize the close connection. The same stresses and hostilities which divide society divide our own souls. The estrangement from which we suffer and which threatens to destroy us is not merely among or between men; it is within Man. And, we further know, our individual inner conflicts, on the one hand, and all the separations and enmities between neighbors and nations, on the other, are facets of an even deeper estrangement: Man's separation from his true home, his alienation from the Ground and Source of his being, his ultimate loneliness and "lostness," his estrangement from God.

We may attribute this separation to man's own "most grievous fault," to his pride and rebellion, or we may account for it by his having fallen under the control of hostile demonic powers. The Bible thinks of it in both ways, and if we think of it at all profoundly, we can hardly fail to do the same. We are aware of ourselves both as responsible perpetrators of sin (in the sense of willful rejection of God's love, which we know to be the true law of our own life) and as the helpless bondsmen of Sin (in the sense of an alien perverse "Will" which has somehow got access to our souls and forces us to do its bidding). We are both "guilty sinners" and "slaves of sin." But however we account for our plight or in whatever terms we describe it, Man is estranged from God and therefore divided against himself. This is his "fallenness," his "brokenness," his wretchedness, his hopelessness, his desperate, fatal sickness. The recovery of his health, of his own inner wholeness, depends upon his being restored to his true relation to his Creator, upon his being brought home again. Salvation, then, is by definition reconciliation, at-onement. The whole

meaning of the primitive Gospel, the "good news," was that in
Christ God was bringing this reconciliation to pass. This was
his saving action. The New Testament—Gospels and Epistles
—have other things to say, but this is what they chiefly say:
The Shepherd went out into the wilderness to find the lost
sheep and has now brought it back into the fold. The Father
has received and restored the lost son. The Healer has come
"to bind up the brokenhearted" and to cure our enmities. In
a word, God has acted in Christ to "reconcile" us to himself,
to "unite" us with one another in him, and thus to make us
whole.

This reconciliation implies a new existence. This is true
of reconciliation even in its simplest form—that between two
persons. Reconciliation in such a case is not an abstract relation between two discrete individuals; it is the existence of a
third entity, real and concrete, in which both share and by
which each is to an extent remade. Similarly, a friendship
cannot be reduced to the status of a mere abstract relation
between two persons, who alone are real. The friendship
also is real. And conjugal love, far from being simply a
reciprocal attitude or feeling in two separate individuals,
makes itself known as an indubitably objective reality—
between them but also surrounding and pervading them—
a new creation of which both have been made living, growing
parts. So to become reconciled with another is not simply
to take a different attitude toward him or to understand that
he has taken a different attitude toward you; it is to share
with him in a new existence, to belong with him to a new
community—a community no less real because only you
and he participate in it. But if this is true of reconciliation
between two individuals, how much more obviously true it is
of the reconciliation of which the Gospel speaks: the total
and ultimate reconciliation, involving God and man, our
neighbors and our hearts, and indeed "all things in heaven
and on earth"! Such reconciliation means the coming into
being of a new objective order of relationships, a new "body"

—a "body" more inclusive, more enduring, and more significant than any of the other "bodies" to which we may belong. It is just this body which, according to the Gospel, God acted to create in Christ, and all that was said in the preceding chapter about the body of Christ is relevant here.

It is to this body, often under this very aspect, that reference is usually being made when, in the New Testament and in Christian devotional and theological language generally, the preposition "in" is used with such terms as "God," "the Spirit," and "Christ." The phrase "in Christ" is especially important in this connection. It was mentioned briefly in the preceding chapter and has often been used in these pages. The Greek expression is often rendered "in union with Christ" and is taken to refer to an intimate, "mystical," personal fellowship between the believer and the risen Christ. This fellowship is certainly involved, but it is not the basic meaning of the phrase. I am sure we are expected to take the preposition "in" more strictly and naturally, to indicate a *place*—its object being an actual body in which we can be *located,* to which we can belong as parts to a whole. This meaning appears most clearly in Rom. 5:12-19 and I Cor. 15:20-22, 45-49, where Paul sets the state of being "in Christ" over against the state of being "in Adam." "Adam" here quite manifestly stands, not for the "historical" individual as such, but for "natural man" in his corporate existence, made in God's image but captured and corrupted by Sin, estranged from his Creator, and divided against himself. "Adam" is Man in his dividedness, his brokenness, his loneliness. It was as our "representative" that he yielded to Sin, rebelled against God, chose autonomy and "freedom" and therefore conflict and alienation.

It is a commonplace that the myth of Adam's creation and fall was less the *source* of the characteristic Hebrew way of understanding Man than the *product* of an effort to express and convey that understanding: what was *told* as happening to Adam was first *known* as being true of Man. At the same time we must not deny to the myth any effective part in the understanding itself. When Paul says, "In Adam all die," he is doing more than making the simple factual statement that all men die; he is reminding us that men have their existence, not primarily as individuals, but as participants in the corporate existence of Man, God's creature and child, and that human death is an aspect of our human estrangement from God and takes its character from that fact. Without the story of Adam, we could not "feel" this truth precisely as we do. For us, therefore, the myth of Adam's creation, disobedience, and "fall" participates in the existential fact of our broken humanity as certainly as the existential fact gave rise to the myth. It is this reciprocal relation which makes "Adam" so effective a symbol (as distinguished from a mere external sign[1]) of Man in his actual dividedness and loneliness.

But if what Paul means is clear when he says, "In Adam all die," his meaning should be equally clear when he continues, ". . . so in Christ shall all be made alive." "Christ," at least at this point, means "the second Adam." In the Event, God has brought a new humanity into being; in Christ, God has given the race a "fresh start." To be in Christ is to belong to a new corporate reality, a "new Man." This new Man in his full stature belongs to the *eschaton*, the final fulfillment beyond the end of history. But he is already in being, however partially and under whatever limitations. The "new creation" has taken place, and the Church is the historical embodiment of the new humanity. Of this "body" Jesus himself, human and divine, is both head and heart. We have seen that the phrase "in Adam" involves necessarily a reference to the story of Adam himself. It is more obviously true that the meaning of the phrase "in Christ" involves—and involves much more vitally and essentially—not only the *story* of Jesus, but the continuing personal reality of Jesus, in a sense to which

[1] I have in mind here especially the distinction which Paul Tillich makes. See *Systematic Theology*, I, 238 ff.

"in Adam" provides no analogy. When we use the words "in Christ," we are speaking, not of someone believed or reputed to have lived in the remotest past, but of a person known to have belonged to our own history, the remembrance of whom and the reality of whose presence constitute the genius of the Church—a person remembered and known as the very person he was and is, "full of grace and truth." The Church, therefore, is not only the "body" of the *Event,* or the "body" of *God's action,* but in a real and wholly unique sense it is Christ's own body and has its reconciling, uniting character because he himself lives in its life.

The author of Ephesians is speaking of this complete and ultimate atonement when he writes: "He is our peace, who has made us . . . one, and has broken down the dividing wall of hostility . . . that he might create in himself one new man, . . . so making peace, and might reconcile us . . . to God in one body through the cross, thereby bringing the hostility to an end. . . . So then you are no longer strangers and sojourners, but you are fellow citizens with the saints and members of the household of God, built upon the foundation of the apostles and prophets, Christ Jesus himself being the chief cornerstone" (Eph. 2:14-20). In a word, when we speak of God's atoning act in Christ, we are speaking of nothing other than his act in bringing the Church into being. This is the "one body" in which we are "made one." The ultimate reconciliation is objectively present in the Church's existence, and the extent to which we severally know its meaning is the extent of our sharing in the Church's life.

It may be added here that it is this character of the Church which defines its primary mission in the world. That mission, at its most characteristic and most important, is not to *do* something for the world, but to *be* something in the world— namely, the constantly growing sphere of a particular and constantly deepening fellowship. The fuller realization of its own distinctive nature and the fuller discharge of its own distinctive function are really one thing. The Church when it becomes truly and fully itself will be nothing other than the world reconciled and redeemed. The wholeness of the Church is the healing of the nations.

This identification of the locus and medium of God's reconciling act in Christ with the historical Church may seem so strikingly at variance with the facts that something further must be said at once to justify it. Far from "uniting" and "reconciling," has not the Church been, through most of its history, terribly divided, nursing deep animosities within its own life, and also terribly divisive, infecting whole societies with the virus of its prejudices and hatreds? It would be foolish to deny that this is true, and shameful to offer any excuse for it or to try to mitigate in the slightest degree the gross anomaly. And yet we must still make the identification we are discussing. Two closely related considerations are pertinent here.

The first of these is that unless the Church *is* the locus and medium, the embodiment, of God's reconciling work in Christ, that work, so far as we can know, did not take place at all. We have seen that reconciliation always implies the existence of community. If in this case the Church is not that community, one can only conclude that this particular act of reconciliation did not occur, for no other community can be pointed to instead. The Church, in spite of all its sins and failings, is the locus, the only locus, of the Event. Whatever happened—that is, in the way of an actual historical occurrence—happened within the emerging Church. Any effects or consequences of the Event took place only within, and were mediated only through, its existence. If the intention of God's action in Christ was not the bringing of this community into being, then we must say either that his intention failed or that twenty centuries of history have not provided the slightest clue to what that intention was.

The only discernible consequence or residuum of the Event in history is the historical Church. This does not mean that God is enclosed within the Church. How intolerable it would be to think of him so! He is the God of heaven and earth, of all nature and history, and of the infinity beyond both. When we speak of "the God and Father of our Lord Jesus Christ," we are speaking of *this* God. But it is still true that we could not have come to know him from observing either the starry heavens, or the human story, or the human heart. We know him, as indeed we constantly say, only through Christ—which means that we know him only through a particular historical Event, actually present and accessible to us only in the Church.

We may be so impatient with the dividedness and divisiveness of the Church as to be tempted to deny its character as a reconciled and reconciling community. But before we succumb to this temptation, let us clearly see that to make this denial is also to deny that "God was in Christ reconciling the world unto himself." We cannot affirm of the Event what we do not have grounds for affirming in the life of the Church.

Actually, however—and this is the second of the two considerations—we do find the reconciling love of God in the Church. We would not belong to it if that were not true; indeed, we do not really belong to it except insofar as this is true. There is great evil—appalling evil—in the Church, and its history under some aspects is a shameful story. Man's frailty, blindness, and sin have left their marks upon it as upon everything else in which he has been involved— marks the more conspicuous because of the moral pretensions the Church has sometimes made. But faulty and partly evil as it is and has always been, it has actually proved to be the carrier of a love of God which cannot be known except through participation in its life—a love which seems to those who receive it as alone adequate to cover our sins and the sins of the whole world and as alone able eventually to redeem us from their power. I have said that membership in the Church is a sharing in memory and the Spirit; it is also a sharing in love, that is, a sharing in the *receiving* of love, a sharing in *being* loved—and being loved in a unique way, which overcomes our loneliness and estrangement, and with our brethren makes us sons again in our Father's house. We are speaking of this actual experience of sharing in love when we speak of the Atonement.

I hardly need to refer here to the highly distinctive character of this love.[2] It is often said that agape, the term almost always used to designate the love of God in Christ, means (at least in the New Testament) an outgoing, selfless, love, in distinction from other terms, especially eros, the love which desires its object. Many question this distinction, pointing to evidences of desire in agape and of unselfish concern in eros, and insisting that love in any form must in the nature of the case include both elements in some proportion. But such controversies about words do not touch the essential point. The term agape as used in the New Testament does not designate a general category, but a particular, concrete thing. It does not denote a kind or type of love, which can be defined with propositions and thus distinguished from other types; rather, it refers to an actual instance of love. This was the remembered love of Jesus for his disciples, which in the Resurrection and the coming of the Spirit made itself known as the very love of God possessing their hearts. To be "in Christ" was to be a sharer in this love, and thus to be both reconciled and healed. The making possible of this sharing—that is, the creating of this community—was and is the atoning deed of God in Christ.

[2] This has been much discussed. See the article by G. Quell and E. Stauffer on agape in G. Kittel, *Theologisches Wörterbuch zum Neuen Testament*, trans. J. R. Coates, in *Bible Key Words*, Vol. 1 (New York: Harper & Brothers, 1951). See also A. Nygren, *Agape and Eros*, trans. A. G. Hebert (London: SPCK, 1932).

If this is true and the reconciliation in Christ is the actual substance of the new communal life which God brought into being when he raised Jesus from the dead, we cannot locate God's atoning act at any earlier, or indeed at any specific, point within the Event. The Event was the reconciling Event it was, not because this or that happening or feature belonged to it, but because God was acting in the whole of it. This does not mean that the actual contents of the Event have no bearing on this character of it. If Jesus had not been responded to and remembered as the supremely reconciling person he was, an actual bearer of the love of God, it is impossible for us to see how the Event of which he was the center could have been the particular reconciling Event it was. We can go further and say that if there had not been the Cross—that is, if this bearer of the love of God had not been violently seized and brutally done to death—then (again, so far as we can see) the reconciling Event would not have occurred, which is another way of saying the Church would not have come into being. But to recognize this is not to locate the atoning act in either Jesus' goodness or his death. That act took place in the "fullness of time"—as all of God's acts in history do—and therefore cannot be located in any isolated incident or circumstance, no matter how important an element in that "fullness" it may seem to us to be.

This distinction, however, is not easy to maintain, and it is not surprising that in actual fact the Church almost from the beginning associated God's atoning act particularly with the death of Jesus. In view of the fact that its self-knowledge was, as we have seen, characteristically expressed in terms of saga and myth and could not have been expressed in any other way, the story of the Son of God who out of love of us became "obedient to death, even the death of the cross," could hardly have failed to become the early Church's way of conveying the concrete meaning of the reconciliation it knew both as realized fact and as vastly richer promise. This was inevitable, not only because the devastating shock of

Jesus' death had made it the center of his disciples' memory of him, so that thereafter to think of him in any connection was to think first of all of his Cross, but also because his death, objectively considered, would have seemed so perfectly to explain the realized fact of the Atonement, once an explanation was sought.

One does not have to be surrounded by ancient cults of sacrifice in order to feel the truth in the statement that "without the shedding of blood there is no forgiveness of sin." Although we, like the ancients, may not have worked out an adequate rationale of it, we too know the healing effect of vicarious suffering. But here was a community of men and women who found themselves not only sharing in a new and wonderful release from conflict and guilt, knowing a forgiveness so abundant that they could speak of it as "God's love . . . poured into [their] hearts," but also unable to forget the awful spectacle of a "shedding of blood" so anomalous, so incredible, that only some vast, deep purpose of God could conceivably explain it. And what could this purpose have been except the bringing to pass of the very reconciliation and peace between God and Man which they had begun to know?

This does not mean, I say again, that there is no real connection between this reconciliation and the incident of Jesus' Crucifixion. It was not mere fancy which associated this meaning of the Event with this particular incident within it. The death of Jesus had been the actual center of the Event—the point where, the human career just ended, the Resurrection and the coming of the Spirit were about to occur —and was also the poignant focus of his disciples' memory of him. The Cross was the crux, the crisis, the decisive moment, both in the temporal sequence and in the community's experience of its reconciling meaning. The death of Jesus had proved to be in truth a "means of expiation." For it was upon those who stood in its particular shadow that the light shone.

It was as they remembered the Cross that their eyes were opened to the whole meaning of the Event, and the love of God which all the time had been seeking them in Christ finally reached them—healing, and breaking, their hearts.

The story did not always have this form. We have seen that the reality of sin can be felt, not only as guilt which we on our own responsibility have incurred and which needs in some way to be expiated, but also as an alien demonic power which has enslaved us and from which we need to be delivered. So Christ's death was thought of both as a means of expiation, a sacrificial offering, and as a final decisive battle with the Satanic hosts. He was, in one context, "the Lamb of God, who takes away the sin of the world" (John 1:29) or perhaps the great "high priest" entering "once for all into the Holy Place, taking not the blood of goats and calves but his own blood" (Heb. 9:12); and, in the other, the Conqueror of all Man's enemies, disarming "the principalities and powers . . . triumphing over them" in his Cross (Col. 2:15). He was—in these two representations of his death, which the Church made no effort to keep apart—both "saving Victim" and "Redeemer King." But both representations were concerned to set forth the heights and depths of a reconciliation which was one day to comprehend "all things in heaven and on earth" and of which the Church, where alone it was embodied (however partially) in history, was the "first fruits" and the promise.[3]

Earlier I mentioned briefly the objection that the Atonement in Christ can hardly be identified with a community so divided and devisive as the Church, making the point in reply that, despite this difficulty, we do in fact find the Atonement there and that we must in the nature of the case find it there if

[3] A more nearly adequate statement of the way of understanding the meaning of Christ's death which has been thus briefly set forth can be found in my book *The Death of Christ* (Nashville: Abingdon Press, 1958), esp. pp. 127-57, along with references to many of the important books on this theme.

we are to find it anywhere. The perplexing problem, which such a statement may raise, of how we can speak of "the Church" at all, in view of the wide divergences and separations among "churches"—a problem touched on more than once in the course of this book and manifestly of crucial importance—will be dealt with more fully in the next chapter. Meantime, however, two objections of a rather different character need to be considered.

The first of these is that in locating the Atonement in a community we are ignoring the significance of the individual and his experience. My reconciliation, it is held, is a personal relation between God and me. It is I myself in my own existence who in Christ am reconciled to God. On this personal character of the reconciliation I would lay as much stress as any "objector" possibly could. Indeed, I should say that if it should be demonstrated that what I have been saying throughout this book is incompatible with the recognition of the reality and the central importance of the personal experience of "peace with God through our Lord Jesus Christ," then I should need to abandon the whole position I have been defending. The Christian must himself be able to know this peace. He must himself be able to "taste and see that the Lord is good." The reconciliation is a matter, not only of objective fact, but also of individual personal knowledge. This knowledge is immediate and self-authenticating. It does not consist in the assurances of any priest or rest upon the authority of any institution. "It is the Spirit himself bearing witness with our spirit that we are the children of God" (Rom. 8:16). One may recall here John Wesley's familiar description of his experience at the meeting of a society in Aldersgate in London where someone was reading Luther's Preface to the Epistle to the Romans: "About a quarter before nine, while he was describing the change which God works in the heart through faith in Christ, I felt my heart strangely warmed. . . . An assurance was given me that He had taken away my sins, even mine, and saved me from the

law of sin and death."[4] I repeat: no theological understanding of the meaning of the Atonement which does not
allow for, indeed presuppose, such experience could possibly
be true. Our freedom and integrity as religious persons will
not be denied; and, if need be, "Reformation" after "Reformation" will affirm them.

And yet this reconciliation with God, for all its intimate
personal character, has never been thought of, even by those
who have placed largest emphasis on it, as subsisting simply
between the individual and God. It has always been regarded
as having an objective, historical ground. We are thinking
of this ground when we say "through Christ" or "through
Jesus Christ our Lord," or when we refer to him as our
"Mediator." We have seen that this mediatorial "work" of
Christ was in the primitive community associated especially
with his death. But, as we have also seen, the death had
this effect of mediating the love of God, not as the simple
incident in the past it may be conceived to have been in
and of itself, but as it was received, responded to, and understood—that is, as it lay in the memory and the heart of
the primitive Church. In other words, the truly objective
historical ground of the individual's experience of grace was
the coming into being of the Church, in which Jesus and
his death were remembered and his living Presence known.

I should say that this is the objective element in what Paul
calls our "justification." Vincent Taylor and others point out
that "justification" is more than "forgiveness"—the latter
term referring to a personal relation ("reconciliation") between the believer and God, but Paul's term designating a
prior, more objective, act of God on our behalf which makes
this personal relationship possible.[5] Although it is undoubtedly

[4] *Journal of John Wesley,* under date of May 14, 1738. N. Curnock, ed.
(London: Epworth Press, 1938), I, pp. 475-76.
[5] See V. Taylor, *The Atonement in New Testament Teaching* (London:
Epworth Press, 1945), pp. 82 ff.; H. Rashdall, *The Idea of Atonement
in Christian Theology* (London: The Macmillan Company, 1925), pp.
90 ff.

true, not only that Paul affirmed such an act as the objective
ground of a new personal relationship, but also that such an
act must be recognized as having taken place, nevertheless
a serious question can be raised as to the appropriateness of
the term "justification" to designate it. That word suggests
that the prior act of God was a legal or juridical act, some
satisfying of the demands of the law. But given the *love*
of God and the fact that the law, whatever it is, is *his* law,
can anything beyond repentance (which, significantly, Paul
does not speak of) be required, so far as the satisfying of
these demands is concerned? Certainly, Jesus' teachings give
no indication that he thought of God's forgiveness as subject
to any prior legal arrangement. It was a free giving of grace,
conditional only, as in the nature of the case it had to be, on
the offender's willingness to accept it, that is, on his penitence
and faith.[6]

And yet, as I have said, a prior objective act of God must
be recognized as having laid the ground for the individual's
entering into the meaning of what we know as the forgiveness
in Christ; and in retrospect we can see that this is true also
of the forgiveness of which Jesus was speaking, although we
shall not expect it to be explicitly noted in his own teaching.
This prior objective act was not a legal act in some cosmic law
court, any more than it was a military act on some cosmic
battlefield—these are metaphors which bring out true facets
of the meaning but cannot be consistently applied. The objective act was a creative act in history itself, the bringing
into being around Jesus of a new human community in which
the God of grace and truth was able to dwell with men and
where the particular repentance and forgiveness which we as
Christians know became possible and available.

It may seem too obvious, but it is not irrelevant, to observe
that the John Wesley to whom we were listening a moment

[6] For a fuller discussion of my own views on the differences between
Jesus and Paul on this point, see *The Ethic of Jesus in the Teaching of the
Church* (Nashville: Abingdon Press, 1961), pp. 75-80, 97-102.

ago was under the constant influence of the Church, and, moreover, that it was while he was in an assembly of Christians, hearing an explanation of one of Paul's Epistles that the intimately personal experience of grace came to him. It came to him—to him in his own personal existence—but it came to him in a particular situation and context. And although it would be true to say that once it had come it was his own indubitable possession and was not dependent on any external authority, nevertheless it was not unmediated. It came to him through, and in, the life of the Church. Even if it had come when he was physically alone, this would still have been true. What knowledge of "Christ" could he have had by any other route? If one points here to the Epistle to the Romans, one need only reply that this writing of the Apostle reflects the experience of the primitive Church, speaks to the Church out of the Church's life, and that one cannot really hear what it is saying without being, or becoming, involved in the Church's existence.

The alternation, or rhythm, or complementary relationship —say it as you will—between the individual and the community, between the subjective and the objective, is of critical importance. On the one hand, it will not do to say (as some do) that since God has in objective fact reconciled us to himself, it does not matter whether we "feel" reconciled or not; our feelings are irrelevant. On the other hand, we must not become the slaves of our "feelings" (as we are often in danger of doing), constantly observing them in morbid introspection, despairing of God's love and forgiveness when we cannot "feel" the "joy of [his] salvation." Actually, just as it is true that our felt joy could be only a false, a fabricated, emotion if it were not for the objective fact of the Church as the very body of Christ (which exists and includes us, however we may "feel" at any particular time), so it is also true that we could not know ourselves as "very members incorporate" in that body—or know even that such a body exists at all—if there were not times when, as we listen to

Christ's words or partake of the bread and wine of his Presence, our hearts are flooded with the love of God and we know a "peace that passes understanding" and a "joy unspeakable and full of glory."[7]

The Christian who supposes that this "inner life of the Spirit" is not life within the historical community, not only does not recognize the medium through which the concrete reality of Christ was communicated to him, but also fails to see the essential character of the reality itself. When he says "in Christ," he refers, whether he knows it or not, to the Church. The Christian life is a *koinonia*. Being a Christian is being a sharer, a participant. The reality in which the Christian shares is a reality in which others also share and is the reality it is because this is true. Alfred North Whitehead has said that "religion is what the individual does with his own solitariness."[8] There is truth in that statement, no less for the Christian than for every man. Ultimately it is I myself who stand before God. But the God before whom I consciously stand as a Christian, although I cannot sense his presence without knowing that it fills all of heaven and earth, was nevertheless in his particular character revealed only in a communal Event, and continues to be revealed only in the communal existence in which the Event is remembered and in a sense constantly recurrent. We are not less truly or less fully individuals, or less free, for sharing in so rich a common life.

[7] In connection with the passage from John Wesley's *Journal* which I have quoted, it is interesting to note another entry at a later date (Sept. 3, 1739): "I talked largely with my mother, who told me that, till a short time since, she had scarce heard such a thing mentioned as the having forgiveness of sins now or God's Spirit bearing witness with our spirit; much less did she imagine that this was the common privilege of all true believers. 'Therefore,' said she, 'I never durst ask it for myself. But two or three weeks ago, while my son Hall was pronouncing those words, in delivering the cup to me, "The blood of our Lord Jesus Christ which was given for thee," the words struck through my heart, and I knew God, for Christ's sake, had forgiven *me* all *my* sins.' " (*Ibid.*, II, p. 267).

[8] *Religion in the Making* (New York: The Macmillan Company, 1926), p. 16.

"But," the objector says, "God's reconciling work in Christ went infinitely beyond anything this common life contains. God does not belong to history as we do and does not know its limitations. The Atonement made in Christ transcends our historical existence and surely cannot be contained in the historical Church." Admittedly and most manifestly, not only is God not confined to the Church, but his action in history— even his saving and reconciling action—must not be thought of as thus restricted. How rash and presumptuous it would be for us to set limits to the possibilities of reconciling action open to him whose judgments are unsearchable, whose ways are so far beyond our vision or understanding, and whose goodness fills the earth and stretches above the heavens! But if the reconciliation we actually know is the reconciliation in Christ, then it is true to say that we know it only in the Christian community. Those who know it there will be convinced that what they are now experiencing is only a "foretaste" of what God has to give through Christ, an "earnest of [their] inheritance." Not only will they set no limit to the reconciliation God is accomplishing in Christ, but they will be sure that no limit can be set. Love will eventually have its full sway; and in that complete mutuality for which we were made we shall be fulfilled. But this is a matter of hope, and the only ground for it is our present sharing in the life of the Church. It is our knowing "in part" which alone gives rise to the expectation that "we shall know even as we are also known." Whatever God may have in store for us—and we shall be confident that it is beyond our capacity to know, or even imagine—what he now offers us in Christ is offered only through a human Event and a human community.

It is striking that the writer to the Ephesians sees the ultimate redemption of all things, the final fulfillment of God's creative purpose, as being simply the consummation of this same Event, the infinite deepening and extending of this same community. To the scope or range of God's action in Christ he sees no limit whatever. He can speak of "the plan of the mystery hidden for ages in God who created all things" and now to be "made known to the principalities and powers in the heavenly places"—a plan "for the fulness of time, to unite all things in Christ, things in heaven and things on earth." But all this is to happen "through the Church" (Eph. 1:10; 3:9-10). God's action in Christ is finally to encompass all of heaven and all of earth in its healing, reconciling effect; but this consummation will be only the Church fulfilled. In other words, this writer is able to identify with the creating and perfecting of the Church the whole redemptive work of God in the whole length and breadth and depth of the cosmos.

If we are not able to rise to such a view of the Church's destiny, will not the reason be either our failure to enter fully enough into the experience of the reconciling love which God offers us even now within its life, or else our failure to recognize clearly enough that it is there, and only there, that this same love has actually found and healed us?

VI *The Church and Its Norms*

THE ARGUMENT OF THIS BOOK MAY NOW SEEM TO HAVE RUN its course. It began with the statement of a thesis—namely, that the act of God in Christ can be defined as his creation of the Church. It continued with a definition of the essential nature of the Church as a sharing in a common memory and in a common Spirit received and known as the living reality of the very one remembered, so that God's act in creating the Church can also be spoken of as his act in raising Jesus from the dead. We then considered the bearing of this thesis upon our understanding of what have been traditionally called the "person" and the "work" of Christ, recalling finally, in the latter connection, the bold conception of the writer to the Ephesians that it is in the perfected Church that God's whole purpose for the whole cosmos will in the end be fulfilled— "the reconciliation of all things in Christ" will be nothing other than the Church realizing under God's creative hand its true nature and amplitude. Not everyone will agree that our discussion of our thesis has been always leading toward this conclusion, much less that the conclusion implies the thesis itself (as *I* believe it does), but we shall probably agree that no statement of the theological importance of the Church could go beyond what the exalted words of this biblical writer clearly convey.

I have sought to anticipate objections to the argument and

to deal with them as adequately as possible as we proceeded. Two questions already touched on, however, are of such importance that separate and more extensive notice must be taken of them. One of these questions is whether I have not ascribed to the Church an autonomy and authority it does not truly possess; and the other, not entirely unrelated, is whether, especially in view of the separations among the "churches," we can properly speak of "the Church" at all, if by "the Church" we mean (as we must) an actually existing thing. These two questions will engage us in this final chapter.

We begin, then, with the question about the autonomy of the Church. "In emphasizing as you have the importance of the Church, virtually identifying with it the revelation of God in Christ, have you not," someone asks, "attributed to it a kind of absolute authority? Has it not been made its own master and its own judge? In a word, have you not abandoned the Reformation principle that the Church stands always under the judgment of 'the Word'?" I should say emphatically that this is not true. Certainly, it is not true of my intention; and if statements in this book have seemed to lay me open to this question and the criticism implied in it, I shall be as ready to correct them, if need be, as I am eager to clarify them in any case.

"The Word," as I understand that term, can in this connection have any one of three meanings or can involve them all. In the first sense, it is a way of referring to the character and activity of God as Creator, Sustainer, and Redeemer. "The world was created by the word of God" (Heb. 11:3). The Word "was in the beginning with God; all things were made through him, and without him was not anything made that was made" (John 1:2-3). God upholds "the universe by his word of power" (Heb. 1:3).[1] To hear "the word" (as

---

[1] The fact that different Greek terms for "word" are used in these passages does not in my opinion affect the point I am making, whatever significance it may have in other connections.

the prophets did) is to know God's presence, his Spirit. We have seen that the Church knows this presence, this Spirit, as being also the presence, the Spirit of Christ. It is not strange, then, that in the theology and devotion of the Church the exalted Christ has often been identified absolutely with this "Word," and all the divine powers and functions have been ascribed to him. But, even so, "the Word [is] *God*," the personal divine reality upon whom we ultimately depend.

I do not believe that any statement or any omission in this book could possibly leave one under the impression that I do not think of the Church as being entirely subject to this personal divine reality, whether called "God" or "the Word." His Spirit is the breath of its life. In every moment its existence as the Church is dependent upon his creative and saving presence. It expresses its very being in the awed and adoring worship of him. His will is the law of its true life, and his love the only source of healing and hope. When "the Word" is taken in this sense—that is, as a reference to God in his creative and redemptive relation to us—has anything been said to suggest that the Church is not constantly and wholly subject to it? Surely not. "It is the God who said, 'Let light shine out of darkness,' who has shone in our hearts" (II Cor. 4:6). Alone we are an "earthen vessel"; the "transcendent power belongs to God and not to us." We do not worship the Church; we worship God. The Church does not save us; God saves us. Above and beyond as well as in and through the Church—and, for that matter, above and beyond and through every other created thing and every other creative relationship—is God's love and power. And if by "the Word" is meant this divine activity not only may it be said that the Church could not have come into existence without it, but also that we should no longer have any reason for affirming this existence if we should lose the sense of its reality and presence.

The problem begins to emerge when the term is taken in the second sense—namely, as a reference to the particular act of God in history which took place in connection with the career of Jesus, his death and Resurrection. "Have you not," I am asked, "entirely subordinated the Word, in this sense, to the Church? Have you not in effect denied that the revelation of God in Christ took place in a unique occurrence in the past under whose authority (as a historical norm) the Church now stands and has always stood, by which it must be guided and according to which it must be judged? In other words, have you not rejected the Event's priority and decisive normative significance?"

Here again I must say: "I hope not." Surely I do not want to and have not meant to. Actually I want to affirm as vigorously as anyone can both the distinctiveness and the priority of the Event. This distinctiveness and priority are, in my intention, preserved when I speak of the Event as being the "emergence" of the Church, or the "beginning" of the Church, or its "coming into being," or when I refer to it in some similar way. The Event is the moment of the Church's *beginning,* and thus an unrepeatable moment in the past, clearly distinguishable from later moments or periods and possessing unique meaning and authority for the Church. To this moment belong the human career of Jesus, his behavior and his teaching as these were seen and heard, the deepening impressions of him on the part of those who were to become—who, indeed, without knowing it were then becoming—the Church. To this moment belong also his death as its impact was felt, the earliest recognitions of his continuing reality and presence, the first experiences of the Spirit, the initial understandings of the significance of what had been occurring. In a word, the content of this moment, preserved in the memory of the Church and in the documents which the memory inspired, not only represents an element in its past by which, whether it knows it or not, the Church has always been, and (so long as it is the Church) must always be, decisively determined, but also provides the continuing Church with a norm and resource to which it must continually repair. All this can be said about the authority of the Event. But it must also be recognized that, for all its normative value, the Event has no historical reality except within the history of the Church. To regard it as having happened outside the Church or before the Church began is to separate it, not only from the Church, but also from the history to which we belong and therefore from any possibility of our knowing it.

The analogy we considered in the first chapter may again be appropriate—even if, as before, only within strict limits. It was suggested that the American Revolution might be defined as the event in which the American nation emerged as an independent state. So defined, there can be no possible doubt that it occurred and that it was the particular event it was because it is carried, so to speak, in the continuing history of the nation. But this does not mean that the nation is unable to recognize both the autonomy and the normative significance of this event. Americans constantly remember it, acknowledge their dependence upon it, and its authority over them. Americans recall it, to be sure, as a moment in their own past, a moment *which belongs to them* and has its particular character only because it does; but they know it also as a moment to which as a nation *they belong* and which has had its distinctive part in determining *their* particular character; as a moment, moveover, from which they know they must not allow themselves to be separated, whether in forgetfulness or disloyalty, lest they lose their soul as a people. It belongs to American history; but American history also belongs to it. Despite enormous differences—elements in the nature of the Church which make it incomparable and unique —the relation of the Event and the Church can, as regards the point of this immediate discussion, be thought of in a similar way. Event and Church can be distinguished—as birth and life can be distinguished—but they cannot be separated.

Because they cannot be separated, it is impossible to say which is the more "important." It is obviously easy to argue that the Event must be so regarded, since without it the

Church would not have come to be at all. But it is equally clear that unless the Church had come to be, the Event would not have occurred at all. Something would have happened under this hypothesis, but not the Event. Jesus would have been born, but not the Christ. He would have taught wisely and well, but he would not have spoken the words of Christ. He might even have been miraculously resuscitated after his death, but the Lord Christ would not have risen. Those elements in whatever happened in connection with Jesus and his career which entered creatively into, and were absorbed within, the life of the emerging community—those elements, and only those, belonged essentially to "the Event." But to recognize this inextricable interdependence between Event and Church does not mean denying the reality of the distinction between them and the importance of our maintaining it. The continuing Church stands always in and under the power of the Church's initial moment. And if by "the Word" is meant what God did in that moment, then the Word has an inalienable authority for the Church—an authority no less real for being exercised entirely from within the Church's own historical life.

We come to the third sense of "the Word" when we observe that it is because of the decisive significance of this moment that *the Scriptures* have their unique authority and worth in the Church. They are called "the Word of God" because they speak to us directly out of the Event and help indispensably in preserving its identity, integrity, and power. The Old Testament books record the "mighty acts" of the God of Israel and reflect the experience of the ancient Hebrew people in the long course of their covenantal relation with him. The content of this collection of writings had been virtually established within the Jewish community before the distinctive Event of Christ occurred. But in being appropriated and absorbed in the emerging Church, it was placed in a new perspective, reinterpreted, and to a degree transformed. The ancient Scriptures became in one moment a new book—an

THE CHURCH AND ITS NORMS

anticipatory account of the meaning (sometimes even of the facts) of the Event itself. At the same time this meaning and these facts were being freshly recorded in new documents. The making of the New Testament Canon was the process of determining which of these documents could be relied on as doing this faithfully and truly. Whatever may be thought of the adequacy or appropriateness of the formal criteria used in this selection (such tests as apostolic authorship), not to speak of the accuracy with which the Fathers and the Councils applied them, Christians would all agree on the general soundness of the final results. These canonical documents bring us an authentic record of the Event as its impact was first felt, and they serve to place us anew, and again and again, within the sphere of its original vitality and power.

The God who spoke in the Event continues to speak to us in the documents the emerging Church either absorbed into its life or produced out of it. The Scriptures *are* the Word of God. They give us a kind of immediate access to the Event. It would be rash to say what might, or might not, have happened, in the Providence of God, if these documents had not been written or preserved; but it can be said that, *so far as we can see,* the Church could not, without them, have maintained that conscious contact with the Event which is essential to its identity and to its authentic being as the Church.

But, as every student of the New Testament knows, the Event with which these documents thus put us in touch is nothing other than the beginning of the Church itself. They may point to earlier times or to outside happenings, but they actually bring us directly and concretely only the Church as it was coming (or had just come) into being, and they give us the pre-Church past (or the extra-Church present) only as this had been taken up into the Church's new existence. This immediate dependence of the New Testament upon the primitive Church does not invalidate its authority for the later Church, but rather establishes it. For if these documents were not putting us in touch with the beginning Church, they would not be putting us in touch with the Event. We may add that New Testament researches, insofar as they have directly or indirectly the effect of increasing our understanding of the essential and characteristic life of the primitive Church, are of inestimable value, for they are clarifying for us the meaning of the Event. But insofar as they do not have this effect, however interesting they may be and however important from other points of view, they are for Christian devotion and theology quite irrelevant. Because they are not concerned with the life of the Church, they are not concerned with the Event and therefore can neither clarify its meaning nor reinforce its authority.

We conclude, then, that the Church stands always under "the Word" of God in the sense of being subject to his will and dependent upon his grace, of being judged and corrected, of being nourished and sustained by his presence. This "Word," in its distinctive meaning and "tone," was first "spoken" in our history in an ancient Event out of which the Church emerged, and memories and written records of which the Church possesses. Not only may it be said that this Event has normative significance for the Church; one must recognize that the Church would have ceased to be itself if it were no longer ruled by it. But, for all its authority and power for the Church, the Event cannot, even in thought, be detached from the Church. The "Word" God spoke in history was nothing other than the calling of this new community into being.

Before leaving the "objection" we have been considering, let me refer to a similar criticism, which to me is more distressing than any other could possibly be. Occasionally someone has said to me: "You emphasize Event and Church so much and in such a way as to discount the importance of Jesus himself. The supreme personal significance of Jesus has been neglected or denied." To such a critic I can only say: "Is this really your impression? Can you have understood me so? Have I really fallen so far short of saying what I have meant to say? Have I not said that Jesus is our most precious memory, that he is enshrined in our remembrance as greater and more beautiful than we can well imagine a man to have been, surpassing in some respects even the portraits the Gospels give us of him? Have I not said that in him and in what happened in response to him God acted to redeem us? Have I not spoken of him as our divine Lord, the object of our love and adoration, and present to our hearts and in our midst as God's very being? Can more than this be said? Tell me, for I shall want to say it.

"But having said all this and whatever more you may give me to say about his goodness and greatness, his supreme importance in God's purpose and for man's life, his continuing creative and redeeming reality for us—having said all this, I ask you to consider your own situation as a Christian and answer if it be not true: that we remember Jesus because we share in the Church's memory; that what we know as the reconciling act of God in him was the creation around him of the community of love and hope to which we belong; and that we can speak of Christ's continuing presence only because we know the mystery and the glory of the Church's own true life."

We are not turning entirely away from this question of norms for the Church when we consider the second objection: "Where," someone asks, "*is* 'the Church' about which you have been speaking and in which you find such enormous values? What actual existence is being referred to when you use the term? Is there such an existence?"

This question, or series of questions, presents us with a problem of identification, not only supremely important for our argument, but also extraordinarily difficult. Indeed, so obviously important is it that one may be tempted to suspect that only reluctance to come to grips with a question of such great difficulty accounts for its having been left till almost the end of this discussion. Actually, however, the question, although apropos from the beginning, could not have been appropriately discussed till now. For in such a case as this, definition has to precede actual identification—we must know what the Church is before we can even ask where it is to be found—and all our previous discussion has been concerned more or less directly with defining it. The Church, we have seen, is by definition an existing historical community in which Jesus is remembered and his living reality as Lord and Christ is known, in which that reconciling action of God in history which we call by Christ's name is expressed and embodied. It is this community we are asked to locate and identify.

At the outset of our consideration of this problem, it may be well to say again what has already been said several times: that any difficulty we may encounter in identifying the Church must not betray us into a denying of its actual existence— unless we are prepared to repudiate or forsake our whole position as Christians. This is quite as true for those who do not recognize that it is true as for those who do. Some reader may have been reflecting all along: "The fatal weakness in this argument is that the author cannot identify 'the Church,' as he has been defining its nature, with any existing thing. Perhaps 'the Church' in his sense may have reality as something ideal or eschatological; but it is not identifiable in actual history. He is, therefore, talking about something that does not exist. And yet his argument requires the recognition, not only that it exists, but also that it is, for the Christian as such, the only significant existence."

To such a reader, I would say: "You are quite right about the difficulty of identifying 'the Church' in history although, as you will see, I do not regard it as an altogether hopeless task. But what do you propose in its place? The perfect human life of Jesus? His death for us? His Resurrection? But what possible knowledge do you, with your presuppositions, have of any of these? How do you know that Jesus' life was perfect? That his death was for us? That he arose from the dead? Do you say, 'Because the Bible tells us'? How, then, do you know that what the Bible tells is true? If you regard 'the Church' as being a questionable historical fact, what am I to say about the 'facts' you are affirming? Actually, when you affirm them, you are either saying words which have no meaning and therefore no real truth for you, or else you are speaking about realities you have experienced in what I have been calling 'the Church.' There is no other conceivable historical locus of distinctively Christian experience, no other conceivable historical source of distinctively Christian knowledge. To deny the actual existence of the Church would be to deny more than the possibility of our *knowing* God's act in Christ; it would be to deny the very existence of the act itself." In a word, the existence of the Church is given in our existence as Christians. However difficult it may be to locate it—however impossible it may prove to be to locate it precisely—its reality, and its reality as a concrete human community, cannot be denied.

We may approach the task of establishing more objectively the existence of the Church by considering, and recognizing as such, several misconceptions of what this objective existence must be. The first of these has to do with the unity of the Church. In the opening chapter, I referred to our deep concern for this unity and to the reasons for it. The concept of "the Church" implies oneness; without it, we could speak only of "churches." Much more, then, is dependent on unity than the effective functioning of the Church; the very being of the Church is involved. All this is obviously true. But we must not fall into the error of identifying the unity of the Church entirely and decisively with unity in outward form. In order to demonstrate the existence of "the Church" I do not need to point to a single, comprehensive organization of Christians, any more than to demonstrate the existence of Scandinavia means that one must point to a single organization of all Scandinavians. At the present moment in world history "the West" may be said to exist quite without reference to NATO or to any other organizational structure. I cite these analogies only to make clearer the one specific point: that it is a mistake to assume that the oneness which is essential to the existence of "the Church" must consist in an external structural solidarity.

As a matter of fact, no great organized body of Christians has ever consistently made this assumption. Many who regard particular structures and usages not universally found among Christians as belonging to the *"bene esse"* or to the *"plene esse"* of the Church, stop short of declaring them absolutely essential to its bare existence. Even those who find themselves forced to take the position that certain of these structures and usages belong to the very *"esse"* of the Church hesitate to draw the conclusion that in particular places and instances the reality of the Church is unknown if they are not present. Whatever our theory, we find it hard to decide that all those who "follow not with us" in these respects do not belong to "the Church," no matter who or what they may be in other respects or how manifest may be the grace of God toward them and in them. I should say that this is true even of our Roman Catholic brethren, who come nearest perhaps to being rigidly consistent in this regard. Actually, for the most part, we feel "our unhappy divisions," not as separations among "Churches," much less as separations between "us, the Church" and those who do not belong to the Church at all, but as divisions within the Church. In our ecumenical endeavors we do not think of ourselves as trying to bring "the Church" into being; rather, we are trying to set the already existing Church free to be itself more fully; we are trying to implement an already existing unity. Few tasks could be more important and more urgent, but we should be mistaken if we supposed that "the Church" will not exist until it is accomplished.

Another closely related misconception is the assumption that the Church, in order to be "the Church"—that is, in order to be the "body" of God's action in history—must be perfect; and that therefore to demonstrate its existence one must be able to point to such a perfect body. This presupposition, although widely prevalent, has always been without theoretical ground, for, as was pointed out earlier, nothing historical— indeed nothing actual or concrete—can ever be without blemish or flaw. The historical, in virtue of both human finitude and human sin, is by inner necessity imperfect, and to say that God either acted in history or appeared in history in a flawless medium is to deny one's statement in the act of making it. If we really know the Church as the historical body of God's presence in Christ, the presupposition would seem to be denied on grounds of experience as well, for as members of it we are aware of, indeed involved in, a historical existence which is characteristically full of human error and sin but in which, nevertheless, we are confronted, not only with the reality, but also with the "fullness," of "him who fills all in all." We shall not be able to understand how this can be—it belongs to the mystery of God's being and creativity —but we shall not be able to doubt the fact itself. One would suppose, therefore, that the presupposition of a necessary perfection in the medium of God's action in Christ would have been effectively destroyed. Indeed, one might marvel as to how such a presupposition should have established itself in the first place.

It did firmly establish itself, however, and, despite both self-contradiction and the evidence of experience, it persists. It has had a seriously distorting effect upon our attempts to understand and interpret as clearly as possible what God did in Christ. On the one hand, the presupposition has led to the making of false claims for the Church. Since the Church is "the body of Christ" and since *ex hypothesi* such a "body" must be perfect, the Church must be perfect. Those who draw this conclusion will probably acknowledge readily enough that *prima facie* it is refuted by the facts; the Church would appear to be a very sinful, fallible, divided body. Therefore, they will argue, this *prima facie* view cannot be true. They are thus led to seek a meaning for either "Church" or "perfect" (or both) which will enable them to bring "the facts" and the conclusion of their syllogism into some kind of harmony.

This search has led to specious definitions of both terms—definitions which, it is safe to say, we should never have thought of except under the pressure of an assumed theoretical necessity. The Church has been arbitrarily narrowed. Since it must be perfect, its existence is denied beyond the limits of some particular group, for which a certain perfection is claimed. The sphere in which the Church is perfect has been arbitrarily restricted—to cite one example, the pronouncements of only one man are infallible and even these only when he speaks *ex cathedra*. Since its members, both individually and in their mutual relationships, are so far from perfect, whether in goodness or wisdom or knowledge, and since the same can be said of its ministers and leaders, a strong tendency has operated to regard "the Church," not as a concrete human community, but as an ideal or abstract structure, or as a "mystical," "spiritual," entity, in neither case belonging to history at all.[2] In a word, a false preconception of a necessary perfection in the medium of God's action in Christ has led to various rationalizations or denials of the weaknesses and inadequacies in the Church—denials or rationalizations which often fail, I believe, to carry real conviction even with those who feel required by the logic of their position to make them.

[2] In an article by Don Cupitt, "What Do We Mean by the Church?" (*Theology* LXIV, 1961), William Temple is quoted as saying, "I believe in the Holy Catholic and Apostolic Church, but sincerely regret that it does not exist." We are not given the context of this quotation and cannot judge how seriously Temple was speaking or what precisely his words meant. But taken as they stand, whether they truly represent Temple's position or not, they do express a not uncommon opinion: "the Church" is an eternal, a heavenly, an ideal, or a purely eschatological reality. I should urge, on the contrary, that there is no point in affirming the reality of the Church, and no ground for doing so, unless we are affirming its actual existence. The adjectives we apply to it, such as "holy," "Catholic," and "apostolic," either are not properly applicable, or can be applied, in some true and relevant sense, to the actually existing historical community.

But on the other hand, the same "logic" leads others to deny that the Church is really the body of Christ. How can it be, they ask, when it is as grossly evil and errant as it is? Those who ask this question may use the phrase "body of Christ," but they find no meaning in it beyond the obvious metaphorical sense. As a matter of fact, these persons, being Christians, actually share in the memory of Jesus and in the knowledge of Christ which belong only to the historical community. They are Christians in virtue of the fact that they participate in this corporate existence. Christ is in fact accessible to them and present with them there, and only there. In other words, they belong in actual fact to "the body of Christ." But they are prevented from giving due recognition to this fact and from drawing the appropriate conclusions, certainly in part by their assumption that Christ can hardly be identified so closely and (in history) so exclusively with so faulty and broken a body. They are prevented from acknowledging "the real presence" in the sacrament, in which "the real presence" is in fact mediated to them, because they are unable to acknowledge the possibility that God as known in Christ may "really" act in and through an action of the Church. They locate the Incarnation, therefore, simply and only in the individual existence of the man Jesus, to whom they do feel able to ascribe the necessary perfection.

Much in this book has been concerned with the point that the Incarnation does not involve perfection on the human side; indeed, that it cannot. This is true even if one attributes an absolute moral perfection, a complete freedom from sin, to Jesus himself in his own individual human existence. The Church has always felt impelled to do this, although it is noteworthy that in the earliest Gospel, Jesus is represented as denying the ascription (Mark 10:18) and that a later one can speak of him as "growing" in favor with God as well as with men (Luke 2:52). But even the Epistle to the Hebrews, which on the whole, not only is unembarrassed by the fact of Jesus' full and unqualified humanity, but finds tremendous significance in it, while going so far as to say that "in every respect" he was "tempted as we are," nevertheless feels constrained to add, "yet without sin." It is clear that this judgment about Jesus is a theological one. The Gospels, although they bear witness to the supreme moral goodness of Jesus and to his unqualified devotion to the will of his Father, provide no basis for the conclusion that he who "knew what was in man" did not know the inner meaning of man's sinfulness as well as of his finitude. One is more easily able to entertain such a conclusion if one thinks of sin in an individualistic, voluntaristic sense—as conscious and deliberate disobedience or rebellion—than if one thinks of it as the massive wrongness and disorder in human existence as a whole, whether associated with the myth of "the fall," or thought of in some other way. The theological reasons for the Church's unwillingness to admit in Jesus' case even the possible presence of sin in the first sense are obvious: Was he not "obedient"? Did he not "overcome"? How else could be have become the Savior? Furthermore, if it is true, as I believe it is, that the Church has often used the term "sinlessness" to refer to a creative goodness in Jesus which, to those who knew and remembered him, seemed so completely to have filled and possessed him that there could have been room for nothing else, then we can, on the basis of that memory alone, affirm it unreservedly and with the fullest conviction. It is appropriate to ask, however, whether we can regard Jesus as having been "without sin" *in the second sense* without separating him from humanity itself and thus invalidating the whole story of God's saving action in him. Would there have been any point in God's "sending his own Son" at all if he had not "sent" him in "the sinful flesh" which we know and from which we need to be redeemed? And is there any other kind of actual flesh in which he might have been sent in any case?[3]

[3] It is the natural aversion to acknowledging any contact between Jesus and sin which accounts for Paul's actually using the phrase *"the likeness of sinful flesh"* in the passage cited here (Rom. 8:3). For thoroughly under-

But even if we should decide that Jesus was absolutely and in every sense "without sin," we still would not be locating "the Incarnation" in such a perfect existence. For however free from sin and from moral imperfection Jesus may have been, the larger social reality of which he was the dynamic center was certainly not sinless or perfect; and it was in this social reality—the concrete body of relationships between Jesus and his own—that the Incarnation occurred, as we have often seen. Actually, if we could affirm perfection in the locus of the Incarnation, we should have denied the reality of the Incarnation itself. "Incarnation" is "the Word in the flesh"; and the second term in that phrase is as important as the first. "Flesh" means nothing unless it designates man's actual existence. "Incarnation" says, not that the Word has *appeared* in an external human form, but that he has actually become human, that is, become involved, really involved, in the actual life of man—not man as he conceivably might be, or as he may finally come to be, or even as God may be thought of as having created him, but man as he actually is, man of whom, and of whom alone, in all his acts, his feelings, his thoughts, history is made. The mystery

standable reasons (we still feel their force) he shrank from saying that God sent his Son "in sinful flesh," although the whole logic of his position requires such a statement. For how could the Son of God have dealt with sin if he had not come where sin has established itself? How could he have "condemned sin in the flesh" if in *his* flesh there was no sin? And from Paul's point of view, was there any reason for his "coming" or "being sent" at all if he were not to "come" or "be sent" into our actual situation? God might have "condemned sin" while remaining in heaven if it could have been effectively done there. Actually, it could not be done there; man's enemy could be defeated only on the human ground where he had entrenched himself. Therefore the "sending" of the Son. But the whole point of it is lost if he sent his Son into a situation *like* ours, to be sure, but actually *not* ours. If Paul had thought of the "work" of Christ as being merely that of manifesting or unveiling God's reality or "the truth," as the later Docetists did, then he could have afforded to say "the *likeness* of sinful flesh." But conceiving of this "work," not as the *showing* of something, but as the actual *doing* of something, it is dangerous for him to take the step toward Docetism which is involved in this phrase, as also in some similar phrases in Phil. 2:7-8.

of the Incarnation does not lie in the presence of the perfect Word in a perfect body. Insofar as "mystery" implies apparent contradiction, this would not be mystery at all, just as it would not be *history* at all. The mystery, the wonder, of the Incarnation lies in the presence of God's perfect Word in the "body" of our actual, broken life.

All this has been said, or at least clearly implied, in an earlier chapter. Here my only claim is that to demonstrate the actual existence of "the Church" I do not need to point to a community perfect in any sense or under any aspect.

A third misconception which creates an unnecessary hurdle in our present undertaking is the assumption that to demonstrate its existence, we need to be able to set definite limits to the actual Church, to be able to say precisely how far it extends, who is included in it, and who is not. It is obvious that we could not apply such a criterion or test to many of the social existences in which we participate. As a matter of fact, I should have great trouble in saying just who belongs to my own family. "The Church," as we have just seen, is not an organization with its definite list of members; but neither is it simply the aggregate of all the organizations and of all the members named in their several lists. It is a social existence to which organizations and their memberships appertain, but which cannot be defined simply and neatly in terms of them. I should say that "America" stands for such a social existence, as do "England" and "France." Even more clearly "Judaism" does. Here are historical communities, arising in distinctive historical events and developments, conveying distinctive traditions, embodying distinctive cultural patterns, following distinctive ways of life. Who doubts their objective existence, but who will presume to set rigid limits to them? How far does "England" extend and whom does it include? Do only those who were born in England belong to it? Or only those who live there? Or only those who have sworn allegiance to the Queen? And among those who were born and now dwell in England, does it matter that there are some who deeply share in the traditional ways and "spirit" of England, others who participate less fully, and others still, hardly at all? Shall we say that all of these belong to England in some equal or absolute sense?

Again, as often before, we must be on guard against pressing such an analogy too far. My point is solely that a certain degree of indefiniteness as regards the limits of a great social community, belonging intimately and dynamically to history, is quite compatible with the recognition of its full and certain existence. "The Church" does not need to be susceptible of precise definition as regards either its extent or its inclusiveness.[4]

In commenting on these three "misconceptions," I have gone some distance toward identifying the Church. The Church is that particular concrete historical community which emerged in and with those first-century happenings in Palestine of which the career of Jesus was the center. It shared with Judaism in a common heritage and, in its new, distinctive character, was a community (a "sharing") in the memory of Jesus and in the knowledge of him as alive and present in the Spirit; but in the earliest period, no more than now, would it have been possible to point to a single organized body, solid and uniform. It was a worshiping community, and

---

[4] I have not used the phrases "visible Church" and "invisible Church" because I do not find them congenial terms. As ordinarily used, they designate two "Churches," whereas I believe the Church must be thought of as one. If by "the visible Church" one means a "Church" whose limits can be neatly defined and whose members can be precisely identified and counted, and if by "the invisible Church" one means a "Church" whose limits cannot be thus precisely determined, "the Church" can hardly be both. It would need to be either "visible" or "invisible"; and under these conditions, I do not see how we could avoid calling it "invisible." Actually, however, I regard the Church as being a very *visible* reality—an actual concrete, human community with a definite, historically created structure upon which its identity as the particular community it is depends. This understanding, which will already have appeared in these pages and will be further emphasized as we proceed, renders the terms "visible" and "invisible" somewhat misleading in this connection.

the God it worshiped was One God, the God of Israel and also "the God and Father of our Lord Jesus Christ"; but apparently there were few, if any, universally shared *forms* of worship. It was from the beginning interested in understanding and explaining its own life—that is, what God had done in bringing the new existence to pass—but, beyond the affirmation that he had done so and had done so through Christ, and more especially through his death and Resurrection, there was no universal agreement on just how the action had been accomplished. It was concerned with organization for the sake of both maintaining its own life and extending its influence and its borders; but there was no single organization and apparently no generally accepted form of organization. However, despite all the differences in polity, cult, and doctrine, so mightily creative was that fusion of "memory" and "Spirit" which essentially constituted it—or, to say the same thing, so great was "the power of his resurrection"—that the Church was manifestly and indubitably a new emergent in history, definitely and recognizably itself. And not only was its existence unmistakably clear; but its social power, its ability to change the shape or course of history, was also soon apparent.

I have been emphasizing the lack of uniformity—indeed, the presence of great variety in structure and usage—within the primitive Church in order to point up the living, dynamic nature of its unity. But the fact that the new society first took shape in a fairly homogeneous Jewish environment and that whatever forms it might later develop would be adapted, more or less appropriately and effectively, to expressing a common memory, faith, devotion and hope, guaranteed from the beginning a certain degree of similarity in form. Vigorous unifying tendencies within—the very unity strong enough to tolerate diversity would be tending to reduce diversity—and growing hostile pressures from without combined to accentuate this similarity and to move the Church toward formal unity. Modes of worship, formulae of doctrine, and patterns of organization and administration which may always have been characteristic of large parts of the Church tended to become universal, and by the third century the Church was near to being "one Church" in outward form as well as in essential substance. This unity, always precarious, proved not to be permanent. The great separation between East and West, the Protestant Reformation on the Continent of Europe, the separation of the Church in England from the Church of Rome—these are only the most important of many breaches of the Church's solidarity. But these divisions, fatefully evil as they were (although a forced conformity would have been worse), did not destroy the reality and essential unity of the historical community which has persisted from the first century to our own, a living body in which the concrete meaning of God's reconciling act in Christ has never ceased to be conveyed.

This affirmation of the continuing reality of the Church, just as it does not mean the ignoring of deep divisions within its body, does not preclude the recognition of a wide diversity as regards the "churchly" quality of its life. The community (or sharing) in the memory of Jesus and in the presence of God in Christ—the communal responsiveness to the Event— which constitutes the essential being of the Church, may exist in all degrees of authenticity and fullness. As the bodily unity of the Church has been broken again and again, so its spiritual quality has been constantly subject to dilution and corruption. We are often tempted to find some neat correlation between the one and the other—to associate the true quality of "church-liness" with some particular form of Church organization, worship, or polity. But any "little system" of this kind we may devise is shattered when we are forced to recognize Christ's (and therefore the Church's) presence in some unexpected place. I myself have found the distinctive substance of the Church's existence in situations as different as a gathering of "two or three" for prayer in someone's home and the great congregation assembled for Holy Communion before the high altar of some cathedral, and among folk as far apart in organization and custom as congregationalists of various kinds, on the one hand, and episcopalians of various kinds, on the other. In both cases, the essential substance was the same —namely, a remembrance of Jesus become one with the experience of his living presence as Lord and Christ, the very being and action of God—nor was it apparent that this substance was always more truly or more largely present in cases of the one kind than of the other.

A source of no little distortion in our understanding of the Church is undoubtedly our habit of using the word "church" to designate what we also call our "denominations" or "communions." This use of the term is an entirely modern phenomenon. The New Testament and the Fathers do not exhibit anything comparable. The Word "church" was then used in the local sense, in referring to a worshiping congregation, whether large or small, and also in the universal, or Catholic, sense to denote the whole body of those belonging to Christ; but any intermediate use of the term, any application of it in a definitive way to some association of churches, was unknown and, I believe, would have seemed to ancient Christians both unintelligible and utterly anomalous. There were, to be sure, local churches which, sharing in particular ways of worship, or in particular polities, or having a similar historical or cultural background, formed groups more or less definite. It is possible, for example, that in the beginning the Pauline churches constituted such a group; and certainly a little later, churches in various geographical areas did. But no one thought of calling such groups as aggregates "churches." The constituent congregations were "churches," of course; and these belonged to "the Church Catholic"; but they did not together compose a "church" in any less inclusive sense.

We should do well to recognize that this third use of the term, familiar as it is to us, is as anomalous now as it ever was. Those "communions" which refuse to acknowledge the existence of any "Church" except that to which their own congregations belong may be more nearly right than many

Protestants are likely to see. Those bodies are wrong insofar as they limit membership in the Church to their own congregations, but they are not wrong in denying that there can be more than one "Church." If I were a Roman Catholic, I should be right in affirming that the Presbyterian (or other non-Roman Christian) must either belong to the Church to which I belong or not belong to "the Church" at all; but I should be wrong if I did not see that, strictly speaking, the Roman Catholic does not belong to the Roman Catholic "Church" or the Presbyterian to the Presbyterian "Church." Both, if they belong to the Church at all, belong to the same Church—and that Church is neither Roman Catholic nor Presbyterian. Given the way our terminology has developed, we may not be able to avoid using the word "church" as a designation of the organized system of churches, the "denomination" or "communion," to which we may belong; but it will be well for us to remember that, unless we mean to deny the existence of Christ's Church outside the limits of this system or association, this is a basically wrong use of the word. The only "church" to which either Roman Catholic or Presbyterian churches belong is the "one holy Catholic and Apostolic Church," the body of Christ in history. There is not—there could not be—more than one. And it seems to me a manifest fact that both Roman Catholics and Presbyterians (not to mention Lutherans, Baptists, Friends, Eastern Orthodox, and other Christians of many groups), may, and do, belong to it.

But here we come to a question of great difficulty. Does it follow from what I have been saying that the Church Catholic is without bodily structure of any kind? Is "the Church" simply the amorphous aggregate of all who "profess and call themselves Christians," of all who share in the memory and the Spirit of Christ? To this question the answer is obviously No. To give any other answer would be to say that the body of Christ is not a body at all—only a vague "stream" or "movement" in history, too indefinite, unstable, and unsubstantial to carry the meanings and values we have been finding in it. On the other hand, however, it is equally clear that no universally acknowledged forms of polity or worship can be discerned among those whom we nevertheless recognize as belonging to it. Here is our dilemma. How can we think of the Church as definite, consistent, and permanent enough in structure to be the actual historical body it is, but extensive enough in range to include all those who manifestly and indisputably share its life?

The clue to the answer, it seems to me, must lie in the distinction between the objective reality of certain structures in the historical community which have always characterized it and may be judged indispensable to its continuing life as the particular historical community it is—between this, on the one hand, and, on the other, the measure in which these structures and their necessary, constitutive character are recognized and acknowledged by those who belong to it. It does not follow from one's failure to acknowledge the structures that one does not share in the life of the body. But it is just as certainly true that one's being able to share in the life without acknowledging the structures does not mean that the structures do not exist and that one is not in fact dependent on them. An adequate treatment of this distinction would need to show how it applies to various actual situations within the Church; such a discussion is impossible within the limits of this book. I should like to clarify the distinction itself, however, and to insist upon its relevance to the issue we are now considering.

We should recognize, then, the fact and importance of the Church's historic structure. The Church is not simply the aggregate of all its members—anymore than the United States of America is simply the aggregate of all its citizens. In both cases, to belong to the community is to be, in some measure, subject to, dependent on, certain historically created structures which express, conserve, and convey the community's distinctive being. It would be impossible to suppose that the inner vitality of the Church could have persisted from generation to generation with any of its original quality and force without continuing forms to hold it. It is true that if these forms had not been dynamic forms, capable of growth and change, the inner life of memory and the Spirit would long since have broken and destroyed them. But it is also true that without the forms, the characteristic vitality would long since have seeped or ebbed away. The identifying of these decisively significant forms (among the innumerable forms of cult and polity which have been developed in various parts of the Church during its long history) is, needless to say, no simple or easy matter. One cannot make the identification simply by ascertaining what forms actually belong in common to all existing Christian groups—of calculating, so to speak, the greatest common factor among contemporary churches. Nor can it be done simply on the basis of either subjective impressions of value or more objective estimates of actual or possible utility. On the other hand, the identification cannot be based on some theory of innate necessity—as though, by some logic, the Church *had* to have a certain structure.

In the last resort, the identification can rest only upon observation of the actual process of history. Considering the historical Church in its whole course and range, one must ask what forms have in fact distinctively characterized it and have in fact been the bearers of its substance. Agreement in detail on a matter of this kind is hardly to be expected, but we are not without objective criteria. In particular, I should say that the more important common forms developed in the first and second centuries, when the Church, still in its first age, came nearer to the realization of unity in its formal structure than it has ever been since—these forms have, on this very account, a peculiar authority. This authority is confirmed by their uninterrupted, and still continuing, prevalence among the great mass of Christians. They have been the symbols and bearers of the Church's reality and unity from the earliest times till now, and constitute what has actually been the distinctive institutional structure of the historical community.[5]

Discussions of the problem of the normative form of the Church are often vitiated by a failure to recognize that the important thing about this early Catholic structure is not the external forms which comprised it, in themselves or for their own sake, but the concrete meaning the forms had within the historical community. If there were a way in which these meanings, in their particularity and concreteness, could be fully expressed and permanently preserved apart from these traditional forms, there would be no ground for insisting on their indispensability. Baptism and the Lord's Supper, for example, are important elements in the structure of the Church because they stand for the objectivity of God's coming to us in Christ and have been, and are, actual bearers of his grace and power. The Canon of Scriptures has its value both as the normative record of the Event in all its concreteness and as the medium of God's continuing revealing and redeeming action. The ancient Creeds are received and treasured as the carriers and guardians, across the generations, of the Church's consciousness of the reality, the uniqueness, and the abiding meaning and force of what God did in Christ. And episcopacy has over the centuries been viewed and valued, not primarily as an administrative office, nor yet as the locus or channel of some magical potency, but as a symbol and guarantor of the Church's character as a sacramental community and of its unity in space and time (hence the importance of "succession" in the conception of episcopacy). It is these meanings —are they not ways of apprehending one single concrete meaning?—which are the inestimably significant thing, and

---

[5] My argument for this position has been presented elsewhere, and the purpose of this book does not require the repetition of it here. See *The Early Church and the Coming Great Church* (Nashville: Abingdon Press, 1955).

the ancient Catholic structure is important because it has in actual fact expressed and conserved them.

But not all Christians recognize their dependence on this ancient structure (not to speak of its actual presence, however broken or attenuated, within their common life) and, even among those who do, there are disagreements as to what elements essentially belong to it and how these are related to one another in a living pattern. What does this fact mean? What am I to make of the existence of these differences in insight and opinion, and correspondingly in organization and practice, among the churches? Am I to conclude that no structure exists—that is, no definitive, normative structure—that the Church is, as regards form, simply and only what it happens to be, or appears to be, or is thought to be, at any particular time and place? Or, alternatively, am I to decide that those Christians who do not discern what seems to me to be the historic structure of the Church and do not conform to it are *ipso facto* not Christians at all and do not really belong to the Church?

It seems clear to me that I can do neither. I must not fail to recognize that the characteristic life of memory and the Spirit, in which to be a Christian is to share, has come down to us from the ancient past within the body of an actual human community which, in its *wholeness* or as a *total body,* is marked by certain historically created forms or structures without which it could not be the particular community it is. But I must also recognize that it is possible for an individual or a group to share in this life and to belong to this body without adequately acknowledging, in thought or practice, the structural elements which have actually given the body its character and the institutional forms through which the life has actually been conveyed to us.

Some Christians and Christian communities are undoubtedly more discerning in this respect than others, more aware of the importance of historical continuity within the Church's existence and more truly cognizant of, and faithful to, the actual structures which have sustained it and, whether recognized or not, sustain it still. But just as none of us is entirely without discernment, so none of us is perfectly discerning. And what we call the reunion of Christendom waits, certainly in part, upon our learning more, all of us—for there is none of us who has not more to learn—of what the Church most truly is, in form as well as substance, in its real essentials and in its full proportions. The Spirit and—not less surely—the Church's history (in which that Spirit has for centuries been working) will each have a part in teaching us.

But the Church, whose nature we shall then better understand, will not have been brought into being by our understanding. The Church is *here,* an objective historical fact. Its actuality is given in our existence as Christians. We may have difficulty in identifying the objective fact, and we may differ in our ways of doing so. But the affirmation of the fact itself is implicit in every expression of Christian devotion and in every confession of Christian faith. And what is affirmed is an existence, not only wide enough to include all who in fellowship have remembered the Lord Jesus and have "loved his appearing"—the "blessed company of all faithful people" —but also definite enough to be called "the household of God, built upon the foundation of the apostles and prophets, Christ Jesus himself being the chief cornerstone, in whom the whole structure is joined together and grows into a holy temple of the Lord, . . . a dwelling place of God in the Spirit."

There is no way to exaggerate the importance of this existence. We may in our pride or error conceive of the Church too narrowly, but we cannot think of it too highly. This human community, belonging fully to our human history, marked by our frailty and sin, is yet "God with us." The corporate reality of the Church is nothing less than the reality of Christ in history, the body of God's action in him.

Nor can we set too high a value on its meaning for us—on what God gives us there. For it is because we have been made "members incorporate" of the living body of the Church that "all things are [ours]"—really ours—"things present," "things to come," and also, just as certainly, things which happened long ago. Jesus is present there as our living Lord, and God's revealing, reconciling, saving action through him is occurring there. The Church is the "new creation," the miracle of the actual coming among us of the "God and Father of our Lord Jesus Christ." And to share in its substance is to find our food and our drink, our work and our rest, our home and our hope.

A Bibliographical Note

THE CONTROVERSY AROUND RUDOLF BULTMANN HAS produced an enormous literature, and it is rapidly growing. Much of this literature is concerned with what has become known as "demythologizing" rather than with the problem of the "historical Jesus" as such; but the line is not easy to draw. I cannot claim to have read all the relevant material even on the latter theme, and I list below only those books and articles which I have actually seen. With regard to this controversy, I need only say that as between Bultmann and his principal critics there is no doubt that I find myself closer to him. I only hope that I have not misunderstood him at the points where I take issue with him, or where, at any rate, I would state both the questions and the answers somewhat differently.

Works of Bultmann. Here I would cite *Jesus* (Berlin: Deutsche Bibliothek, 1929; Eng. tr., Louise Pettibone Smith and Erminie Huntress Lantero, *Jesus and the Word* [New York and London: Charles Scribner's Sons, 1934]); *Theologie des Neuen Testaments* (Tübingen: J. C. B. Mohr, 1948-53; Eng. tr., Kendrick Grobel, *Theology of the New Testament* [New York: Charles Scribner's Sons, 1951-55]); *Glauben und Verstehen*, II, (Tübingen: J. C. B. Mohr, 1952; Eng. tr., J. C. G. Greig, *Essays, Philosophical and Theological* [London: SCM Press, 1955]); "Die Entmythologisierung der Neutes-

149

tamentliche Verkündigung als Aufgabe," in Hans Werner Bartsch, ed., *Kerygma und Mythos* (Hamburg: Reich, 1951-52; Eng. tr., Reginald Horace Fuller, *Kerygma and Myth* [London: S. P. C. K., 1953]); "Allegemeine Wahrheiten und Christliche Verkündigung," *ZTK*, Vol. 54, 1957; *Jesus Christ and Mythology* (New York: Charles Scribner's Sons, 1958); *Das Verhältnis der urchristlichen Christusbotschaft zum historischen Jesus* (Heidelberg: Carl Winter Universitätsverlag, 1960; privately translated by Norman Perrin).

Works of Interpreters and Critics. Among these, arranged in approximately chronological order, may be mentioned: Ernst Käsemann, "Das Problem des historischen Jesus," *ZTK*, Vol. 51, 1954; Friedrich Gogarten, *Entmythologisierung und Kirche* (Stuttgart: Vorwerk-Verlag, 1953; Eng. tr., Neville Horton Smith, *Demythologizing and History* [New York: Charles Scribner's Sons, 1955]); Nils Alstrup Dahl, "Der historische Jesus als geschichtswissenschaftliches und theologisches Problem," *Kerygma und Dogma*, I, 1955; Ernst Fuchs, "Die Frage nach dem historischen Jesus," *ZTK*, Vol. 53, 1956; Günther Bornkamm, *Jesus von Nazareth* (Stuttgart: Kohlhammer, 1956-57; Eng. tr., Irene and Fraser McLuskey and James M. Robinson, *Jesus of Nazareth* [New York: Harper & Brothers, 1960]); Joachim Jeremias, "Der gegenwärtige Stand der Debatte um das Problem des historischen Jesus," *Wissenschaftliche Zeitschrift der Universität Greifswald*, VI, 1956-57 (Eng. tr., *Expository Times*, Vol. 69, 1958); Ernst Käsemann, "Neutestamentliche Fragen von Heute," *ZTK*, Vol. 54, 1957; Hermann Diem, *Der irdische Jesus und der Christus des Glaubens* (Tübingen: J. C. B. Mohr, 1957); Ernst Fuchs, "Glaube und Geschichte im Blick auf die Frage nach dem historischen Jesus," *ZTK*, Vol. 54, 1957; Paul Althaus, *Das sogennante Kerygma und der historische Jesus* (Gütersloh: C. Bertelsmann, 1958; Eng. tr., David Cairns, *Fact and Faith in the Kerygma of Today* [Philadelphia: Muhlenberg Press, 1959]); Gerhard Ebeling, "Die Frage nach dem historischen Jesus und das Problem der

Christologie," *Wort und Glaube* (Tübingen: J. C. B. Mohr, 1960); Oscar Cullmann, "Out of Season Remarks on 'the Historical Jesus' of the Bultmann School," (Eng. tr., J. Louis Martyn), *Union Seminary Quarterly Review,* Vol. 16, 1961.

Belonging also within the context of this discussion are James M. Robinson, "The Historical Jesus and the Church's Kerygma," *Religion in Life,* Vol. 26, 1956-57; John Macquarrie, *The Scope of Demythologizing* (London: SCM Press, 1960); William R. Farmer and Norman Perrin, "The Kerygmatic Theology and the Question of the Historical Jesus," *Religion in Life,* Vol. 29, 1959-60; William R. Farmer, "On the New Interest in Jesus," *The Perkins School of Theology Journal,* 1960; Hans Werner Bartsch, "The Still Unfinished Debate on Demythologizing," *Religion in Life,* Vol. 30, 1961; Schubert M. Ogden, *Christ Without Myth* (New York: Harper & Brothers, 1961). See also James M. Robinson, *A New Quest of the Historical Jesus* (London: SCM Press, 1959), which makes not only a very discerning report on the German discussion, but also a significant contribution of its own to it. Outside of this particular discussion as such, but closely relevant to the more basic problem of the relation of faith and history, is Richard Reinhold Niebuhr, *Resurrection and Historical Reason* (New York: Charles Scribner's Sons, 1957).

Books on Christology and the Church. At the end of my book *Christ the Lord* (1945) I gave a highly selective, but fairly adequate, bibliography on christology. To this list additions now need to be made, some new books and others I had overlooked: notably, Lionel Spencer Thornton, *The Incarnate Lord* (London: Longmans, Green & Co., 1928); Emil Brunner, *The Mediator* (London: Lutterworth Press, 1934); John Wick Bowman, *The Intention of Jesus* (Philadelphia: The Westminster Press, 1943); Floyd Vivian Filson, *One Lord, One Faith* (Philadelphia: The Westminster Press, 1943); Rudolf Bultmann, *Theology of the New Testament* (Grobel translation, already cited); George Simpson Duncan,

Jesus, Son of Man (New York: The Macmillan Company, 1949); Thomas Walter Manson, *The Servant-Messiah* (Cambridge: Cambridge University Press, 1953); Reginald Horace Fuller, *The Mission and Achievement of Jesus* (London: SCM Press, 1954); Paul Tillich, *Systematic Theology*, II (Chicago: University of Chicago Press, 1957); Cyril C. Richardson, *The Doctrine of the Trinity* (Nashville: Abingdon Press, 1958); Oscar Cullmann, *The Christology of the New Testament* (Philadelphia: The Westminster Press, 1959); and W. Norman Pittenger, *The Word Incarnate* (New York: Harper & Brothers, 1959).

As regards the theme of the Church, again I cannot more accurately indicate the modern books upon which I have been most dependent than by referring to the bibliographical notes in an earlier work—this time *The Early Church and the Coming Great Church*. To the titles named there I would add Charles Clayton Morrison, *What Is Christianity?* (New York: Harper & Brothers, 1940); Eric Lionel Mascall, *Christ, the Christian and the Church* (London: Longmans, Green & Co., 1946); Ernest Best, *One Body in Christ* (London: S. P. C. K., 1955); Anders Nygren, *Christ and His Church* (Eng. tr., Alan Carlsten; Philadelphia: The Westminster Press, 1956); Claude Welch, *The Reality of the Church* (New York: Charles Scribner's Sons, 1958); and Paul S. Minear, *Images of the Church in the New Testament* (Philadelphia: The Westminster Press, 1960).